THE THIN VEIL OF LONDON

THE THIN VEIL OF LONDON

RICH COCHRANE & ROBERT KINGHAM

London photographs by ALASDAIR MACKENZIE

Map illustrations by GABY KINGHAM

minimumlabyrinth.org

Frontispiece: detail from cast-iron water pump in Queen Square, dated 1840

First published by Minimum Labyrinth in 2013
Copyright © Rich Cochrane and Robert Kingham 2013
Reprinted 2023 and bound by Lulu Press, Inc.

London photographs (frontispiece, pp 27, 37, 39, 55, 63, 116, 128, 130)
© Alasdair Mackenzie 2013
Cover photograph © Robert Kingham 2013
Map illustrations © Gaby Kingham 2013
All other images: Creative Commons

Rich Cochrane and Robert Kingham have asserted their rights under the
Copyright, Designs and Patents Act 1988 to be identified as the authors of this work

ISBN: 978-1-312-65712-0
Imprint: Lulu.com

CONTENTS

Introduction • 10

THE GLASS HARMONICA • 14

THE TRIBES OF EUROPE • 46

INSIGHT • 78

ECSTASY IN SUBURBIA • 108

Bibliography • 132

For

Clare and Gaby

psychogeographers' widows

*When the next morning I came down, I found Professor Gregg
pacing the terrace in his eternal walk.*

*"Look at that bridge," he said, when he saw me;
"observe the quaint and Gothic design, the angles between the arches,
and the silvery grey of the stone in the awe of the morning light.
I confess it seems to me symbolic; it should illustrate a mystical allegory
of the passage from one world to another."*

*"Professor Gregg," I said quietly,
"it is time that I knew something of what has happened,
and of what is to happen."*

ARTHUR MACHEN, The Three Impostors,
'The Novel of the Black Seal'

INTRODUCTION

Time may be linear but history is not. Trying to make sense of it often feels like riding on the shuttle of a loom, propelled by a mad weaver, flying back and forth looking for connections between the echoes and fragments that make up the raw material. The history of ideas, in particular, resembles a basket of wool that the cat has got into, and the best one can do is to indicate a few places where threads of particular colours appear and disappear. Looking for a grand structure or greater purpose in it is a lifetime's work, and can be fruitless or even ridiculous: in attempting to get comfy, the cat has been rearranging it for the last three thousand years.

This book emerged from a series of walking tours of Holborn and Bloomsbury that we performed in 2013 in collaboration with the Museum of London. These were part of the 150th birthday events for Arthur Machen, the Welsh writer whose sense of the mystical was woven into the warp and weft of the streets of London. We quickly realised that there was more that we wanted to say than could be stuffed into a two-hour walk, and that a book was needed for us to engage with the ideas thrown up by Machen's books and by the local history we found.

So what is this book? It is not a literary-critical account of Machen's work; there are already plenty of those. Nor is it, primarily, a tour guide: David Hayes's *East of Bloomsbury* (1998) tells a comprehensive history of these streets and has been an invaluable source, as has UCL's online Bloomsbury Project, led by Rosemary Ashton and Deborah Colville in the late 2000s. *The Thin Veil of London* seeks to present some of the intellectual background that informed Machen's writing at the turn of the last century and the philosophical problems that his writing throws up for us in the present.

In particular, we were intrigued by what at first appear to be two quite separate themes threading through his work. Machen's stories teem with sinister ancient pre-Christian horrors – troglodyte races and malevolent fauns – that lurk just beneath the surface of modern life. Yet at the same time, there are glimpses of a positive theology that invite the visionary to step through the veil of illusion into another world – a magical world; what Machen called 'the eternal beauty hidden beneath the crust of common and commonplace things; hidden and yet burning and glowing continually if you care to look with purged eyes'. Sometimes the lifting of the veil occurs on an ancient tumulus in the Welsh countryside of his childhood; often it can be found in a back street of London. These two themes make up what he called 'the pattern in his carpet'. But perhaps they are one theme: two sides of the same coin, the same Gold Tiberius, flung in terror by the young man in spectacles and ricocheting off the walls of London alleys down through time.

In Machen's stories, coins and artefacts disappear into the unknowable darkness of the city and later come to light. We have found that ideas, too, run out of sight for a while before re-emerging in unexpected places. Perhaps, because we are cautious about building grand structures out of them, this book is more of a geography of ideas than a history. In his third Seminar, the twentieth-century psychoanalyst Jacques Lacan referred to certain fixed points in the otherwise 'shapeless mass of stuffing' that is the human mind: *points de capiton* ('upholstery buttons') that hold things together and ensure that at least in some cases words really mean what they are supposed to mean.

We have identified a few of these *points de capiton* in the centuries of shapeless history we consider; indeed, much of what follows can be seen as a kind of cartography of these points. They pull and hold together what would otherwise look like meaningless rags and stuffing, making contact with the streets and buildings of Holborn and Bloomsbury, each gathering into itself a theme from Machen, whether a pattern in the carpet of his stories or a throwaway remark. In doing so they create a kind of structured space in which the voices of the writer and his contemporaries can be heard more clearly. This is, then, not a work of literary criticism but an opening-up of the possibility of a reading. This space, however, is a temporary one; a sideshow booth that will be disassembled once you have bought and drunk our snake oil. Then history will be unbuttoned again.

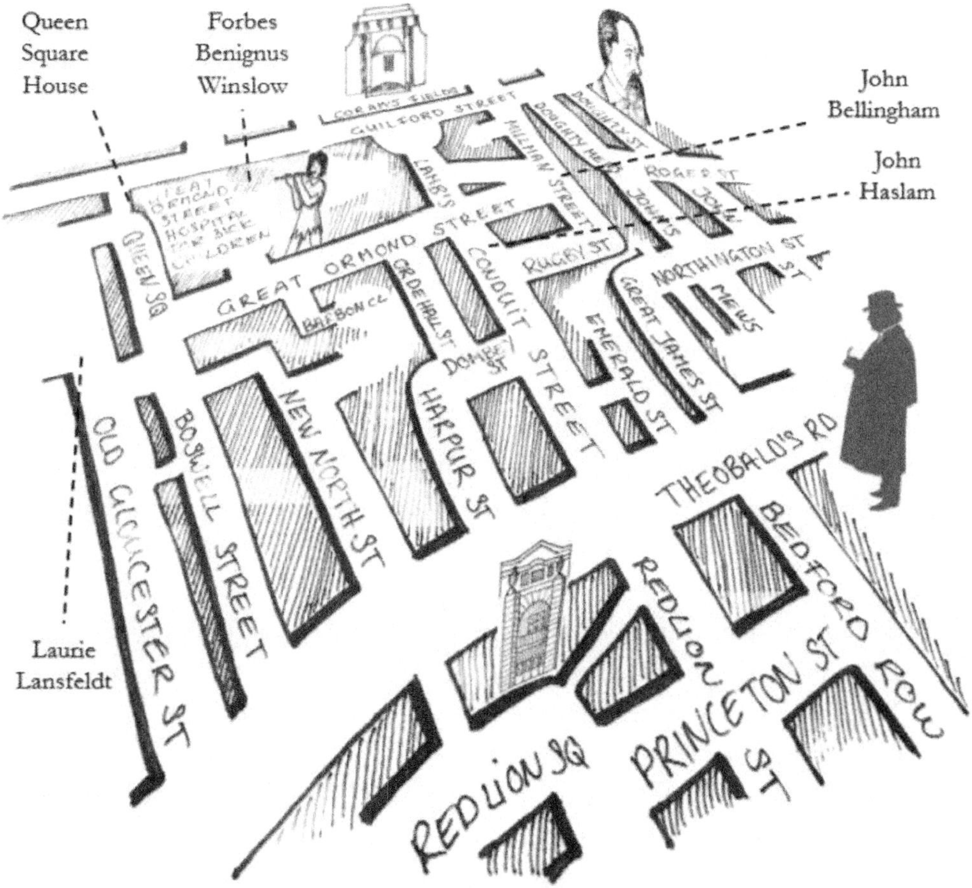
Queen Square House
Forbes Benignus Winslow
John Bellingham
John Haslam
Laurie Lansfeldt
CORAM'S FIELDS
GUILFORD STREET
GREAT ORMOND STREET HOSPITAL FOR SICK CHILDREN
QUEEN SQ
LAMB'S
MILLMAN STREET
DOUGHTY MEWS
DOUGHTY ST
ROGER ST
JOHN'S
GREAT ORMOND STREET
CONDUIT STREET
RUGBY ST
NORTHINGTON ST
MEWS
GREAT JAMES ST
EMERALD ST
BARBON CL
ORDE HALL ST
DOMBEY ST
HARPUR ST
NEW NORTH ST
BOSWELL STREET
OLD GLOUCESTER ST
THEOBALD'S RD
BEDFORD ROW
RED LION ST
PRINCETON ST
RED LION SQ

THE GLASS HARMONICA

It was 15 May 1800 and the royal family was watching a performance of *She Would And She Wouldn't*. The play was an old one. Most English theatre at that time was a moribund treadmill: crass revivals of sentimental comedies sure to pack out three-thousand-seat playhouses. So nothing remarkable was happening on-stage. The performance is remembered only for the drama that took place in the auditorium. While the king was acknowledging the audience's applause from the royal box, a man named Hadfield pulled out a pistol and took a shot at him.

James Hadfield had no particular desire to murder King George III. Indeed, he did his best to make this clear at the time. Before he shot (and missed) him, he shouted "God bless your Royal Highness; I like you very well, you are a good fellow". Rather, he had come to believe that he was Christ, returning to bring about the end of days, and therefore he must be sacrificed so as to absolve the sins of the world. However, suicide being a mortal sin from which repentance is impossible, he had decided to make the hangman his proxy by committing high treason. It is not known whether he missed with his bullet intentionally, since to compass the death of the king was sufficient to secure a death sentence.

Hadfield was not hanged. Unfortunately for him (and perhaps for humanity's redemption) his lawyer was the brilliant Thomas Erskine. Erskine pointed to the contradictions in Hadfield's actions as a mark of insanity, caused by a bayonet wound sustained in France that had 'cut across all the nerves which give sensibility and animation to the body'. Those who were clearly raving mad – cases of total and complete loss of memory and understanding – had long been exempted from ordinary punishment. Hadfield, however, was evidently very far from that. The prosecution had already driven home the apparent normality of his behaviour and the obvious premeditation of his action, both of which pointed away from either congenital or temporary madness. Erskine's defence marked him out as a product of the eighteenth century. He argued that

> it is the REASON OF MAN which makes him accountable for his actions; and the deprivation of reason acquits him of crime.

Note the emphasis on deliberative rationality, in contrast to mere will. It seems that others of Erskine's Enlightenment predisposition were present, because the jury found Hadfield 'not guilty'. This was a modest landmark in legal history: not the first time such a verdict had been handed down, but the first time the plaintiff had been so in control, to all appearances, of his faculties. In recognising a kind of localised madness, it marked a moment at which the insane ceased to be a species set apart from ordinary humanity. Hadfield's act was the rational consequence of an irrational premise. How many of us can be sure we do not harbour such premises of our own?

The immediate problem posed by Hadfield's conviction was what to do with him. Since he had been judged insane, he would be committed to an asylum, yet asylums tended to discharge their patients once they had regained lucidity. This policy often led to the release of dangerous inmates who were experiencing a temporary remission. Hadfield was already lucid, which would effectively trigger his immediate release. Parliament had to step in with the hurriedly-constructed Criminal Lunatics Act, retrospectively defining a verdict of 'not guilty by reason of insanity' which enabled him to be incarcerated for life in Bethlem Hospital.

The legal and practical complexity of dealing with the mad meant that the subject attracted the latest scientific theories and the fashionable philosophies. Thus, madness becomes a barometer for the age. There had been a book published seventy years before, in 1733, entitled *The English Malady*. In the jargon of his time, its author, George Cheyne, was an 'iatromechanist'. This was a new, rigidly mechanical application of physics to medicine, and in some areas it met with success, such as John Mayow's discovery of the life-sustaining properties of what we now call oxygen. Iatromechanists believed the body to be a simple machine, entirely separate from the soul, and to explain the difference between a living creature and a corpse, they tended to posit a physical 'life force', on the model of Newton's gravitational force. Electricity seemed a promising candidate for this life force: as Luigi Galvani discovered in 1771, it had the ability to make severed frogs' legs twitch. Fifty years later, the electricity of a lightning bolt animated Frankenstein's monster. Although he was not a card-carrying iatromechanist, the most famous eighteenth-century proponent of this kind of theory was Mesmer, who called his life force 'animal magnetism'. Franz Anton Mesmer's theories are a curious mixture. They reflect the cutting-edge science of the time but also are imbued with sympathetic magic, where one object affects another at a distance through 'sympathy' or similarity: effigies, Voodoo dolls, horcruxes. This was not just the stuff of superstition. In the Renaissance this was found in some of the speculations of Robert Boyle, a virtuoso of the Royal Academy, who investigated many phenomena including alleged supernatural occurrences. In his *Essay of the Great Effects of Even Languid and Unheeded Motion* (1685) he writes of the effect of the folk dance called the *tarantella* on the soul, by which it was held to cure spider bites, and of the possible magnetic attraction between the philosophers' stone and angels.

Mesmer conjectured that gravitational effects must be transmitted like waves through a sort of fluid medium. In itself this was not controversial – it had precedents going back at least as far as Paracelsus and Fludd but was also a standard theory among those who resisted the notion of the vacuum. Although the existence of the vacuum had been demonstrated by Boyle and others, the notion of an interplanetary fluid medium, the æther, remained a standard explanatory device in science until the Michaelson-Morley experiment of 1887 provided strong evidence against it; indeed, it continued to be more or less respectable until the implications of Einstein's special relativity had been fully digested. Newton and Kelvin believed in a gravitational æther more or less like Mesmer's. It seemed to Mesmer that the movements of the æther, caused mostly by the planets but also by everything else that moved within it, must have an effect on the human body, and hence the emotions, and other aspects of psychology. He called this 'animal gravitation'. The word 'animal' here relates to the Latin *anima* (mind, or soul) rather than being anything to do with animals as such. This is the audacious part of his theory, but at first glance it sounded similar to Galvani's then-respectable notion of 'animal electricity' as a life force.

Mesmer became in-demand as a physician but his appearances before the French Academy of Sciences failed to impress the *philosophes*, who took him for a charlatan. It didn't help that he was tremendously successful, claiming to cure a huge range of diseases for the rich and powerful across Europe. Rejected by the scientific establishment, mesmerism drifted into circles in which the esoteric was tolerated. Indeed, it moved so far into those circles as to become a kind of secret society in itself. Following the model of Freemasonry, Magnetic Societies sprang up in France and Belgium, requiring initiation, offering medical treatments and pursuing typically liberal-Enlightenment social reforms. All of this was to the dismay of Mesmer, who clung to the hope that his discovery would be accepted by the scientific community, and he disowned the esoteric societies that had laid claim to his 'discovery'. It was too late.

The Marquis de Puységur, founder of one of these groups, seems to have succeeded in inducing somnambulism. Subsequently he and his circle found that they could talk with their subject while apparently in a sleeping state: in this way they stumbled upon hypnotism. Today this is a recognised phenomenon, although the mechanism by which it works is still not well-understood. To the scientific establishment of the 1780s, however, it must have looked like sheer flim-flam. To those of an esoteric bent the trance-state offered the possibility of experiencing visions and communing with spirits at will, rather than hoping to be chosen by God. Prophesying, automatic writing, clairvoyance and audiences with angels and even the Virgin Mary were reported. Some practitioners found that they could dispense with magnets and other accoutrements and become 'spiritists'. In a sense, Mesmer's failed scientific theory had given birth to a technology of trance, a manufactory of mysticism that was entirely independent of it.

By the early nineteenth century, perhaps surprisingly, animal magnetism had become a respectable field of study at German universities. Forces like magnetism and electricity were little-understood but jibed well with the organicism, vitalism and cosmic holism of Goethe's ideas about science and those of his Romantic followers. Developing a theory of psychology was considered an important project and many attempts were made on it. Animal magnetism thereby received a new lease of scientific life. On its descent from the academy to the sideshow, mesmerism offered cheap thrills and convenient narrative possibilities to the writer of Gothic fiction. Laurie Lansfeldt, who lived at 2 Queen Square, wrote a novel entitled *Unknown to Herself*, whose heroine is mesmerised into marrying a man. There are hints of the practice all over the tradition, notably in Hawthorne's *House of the Seven Gables*, Stoker's *Dracula*, and perhaps even in the 'glittering eyes' of the narrator of Coleridge's 'Rime of the Ancient Mariner'. Once it was entirely abandoned by science, mesmerism became available for more esoteric or whimsical applications. It offered an analogue for the dream-state, in which the subject becomes something other than themselves. This is again a form of ecstasy, that offers more than a convenient plot device: it paints an unnerving picture of the vulnerability of the self, especially the self-without-will, which is also a self-without-morality. Yet it also offers a tempting escape route from the relentlessness of being a self at all. As with opium, so with the altered states induced by the mesmerists.

When he failed to gain acceptance amongst the mainstream scientific community, Mesmer found himself more and more in demand as a healer. He held gatherings in which the rituals he devised were enacted to the eerie keening of the glass harmonica. It was at one of these gatherings that Mozart first heard the instrument's unusually pure, penetrating tone, and he subsequently wrote music for it. Mesmer was following an established tradition of musical therapy: as early as 1677 an experimenter in Nürnberg claimed that different pitches, produced by rubbing the rims of glasses, could agitate the emotions and even have physiological effects such as thinning the blood. The theory draws on much older medical theories of cosmological correspondence: the 'four humours' predicted that the ailing body could be affected by heat and moisture, foods and drinks, stones and stars. Why not music? After all, these theories were rooted in a kind of Pythagorean numerology that made a fetish of the simple ratios of musical harmony and extrapolated them to other, apparently similar forms of correspondence.

It's tempting today to dismiss Renaissance science and medicine as a childish hotchpotch taken from ancient books, a morass of superstition and a wild mania for order; the world of John Dee and Nostradamus. Yet it is important to remember that this tradition directly produced Galileo, Kepler and Boyle, and that it deeply influenced Newton. The 'scientific revolution' of the seventeenth century was no such thing; it was a slow, organic development from the now-mocked thought of the previous century, without which it probably could not have existed. Even in the eighteenth century the physical sciences remained speculative, with many forces, entities, substances and principles conjured into existence simply because they seemed necessary for a theory to be developed at all. Newton's 'gravitational force' is only the most famous such example: nobody in his time or Mesmer's had any idea what this force might be, or any way to make a direct observation of it; all they had was a system that presumed it, and which, on that basis, seemed to fit the facts remarkably well. Over time the philosophy of science has become reconciled to such postulates, but only at the expense of a less ambitious sense of what science can be: not a full and final account of how the universe is but a pragmatic machine for making and refining predictions.

So it was not extravagant for Mesmer to lay claim to his own force: it was a recognisable 'life force' of the kind that had been in the tradition since Plato and Aristotle were grafted onto Western thought. This tradition holds that there must be an 'animating principle' that enables people, cats and even plants to move themselves around in a way that is denied to rocks. In Plato it is a sort of political structure, a system of government in which three branches are held in balance: physical desires are opposed to both rationality and what would later be described as a 'conscience' that attempts to enforce moral goodness. Plato's student, Aristotle, also posited three branches to the soul, although these are more taxonomic than administrative: the 'vegetative soul' that allows an object to grow, the 'animal soul' that allows it to move around, and the 'rational soul' that allows it to direct its movements through reason. The last, of course, is possessed only by human beings. In Greek the word for all this is *psyche*. Mesmer positioned his own psychological theory as a complement to Newton's gravitational force and hoped that it would achieve the same scientific respectability, and that it would make Mesmer a *philosophe*, a man of the Enlightenment.

But it was not to be. Committee after committee left him out in the cold. In his capacity as the United States Minister to France, Benjamin Franklin participated in a distinguished panel tasked with assessing the scientific merit of Mesmer's practices. Their report of 1784 declared that any positive effects of his therapies were the result of 'auto-suggestion' – what we would today probably call the placebo effect – and had no basis in recognisable science. So Mesmer returned to his magical-scientific theatre, aided by the numinous ambience of the glass harmonica, an instrument which in a mild twist of irony had been invented many years earlier by Benjamin Franklin.

The hunt to identify the 'life force' continued, gradually converging with increasing knowledge of the nervous system. The association of mental functions with the nerves was not new. The nervous system was discovered by Herophilus and Erasistratus, working at the 'museum' in Ptolemaic Alexandria in the third century BC. The leading interpretation among the ancients was that *pneuma* – which may be variously translated as breath, spirit or life force – flowed through the nerves as blood does through the veins. In his autobiography, John Stuart Mill described his 'shattered nerves', which we might today diagnose with the more bland and opaque 'depression', and Richard M. Bucke, whose work was praised by the influential positivist Auguste Comte, argued strongly that it is in the nerves that we can find the moral sense of the human being. In the mid-nineteenth century in Berlin, the physician Wilhelm Griesinger was developing an up-to-date neuroscience centred on the nervous system of the body; he pointed to something else besides the frailty of the nerves which was to blame for the malady of madness – modern life:

> The present state of society in Europe and America keeps up a general half-intoxicating state of cerebral excitement which is far removed from a natural and healthy condition, and which must predispose to mental disorder: thus many become insane.

This theory, of madness as a reaction to modernity, seems to come from a more deeply-rooted anxiety, and as an affliction is difficult to treat. Thus, it resisted medicalisation, and the nervous model of abnormal psychology was not seriously challenged until Freud, for whom the potential for madness lay dormant in all of us. Yet he, too, bore the same influences. In his strict materialism, and in his intention to produce a scientifically credible psychology, he fell back on the language of the iatromechanists to tell his stories. The development of the mind became a kind of hydraulic or electrical circuit for conveying (and damming-up) the energy of the libido (which in itself is another intangible 'life force').

And Freud, too, explicitly indicts the modern world for its effects on the *psyche*, just like George Cheyne had done two centuries before in *The English Malady*. By the 'English malady', Cheyne meant a disease of the nerves or life force. Our modern (and far less materialistic) language might call this a 'mental illness'; yet in our world mental illness affects the individual, and to some degree isolates them from 'normal' society. Cheyne was writing before our notion of 'normality' existed, and so the English malady is not a mental illness in our sense at all. Cheyne saw that the illnesses he described had social as well as mechanical causes. Alongside such environmental factors as the weather, he blames

> the Richness and Heaviness of our Food, the Wealth and Abundance of the Inhabitants [of England] (from their universal Trade) the Inactivity and sedentary Occupations of the better Sort (among whom this Evil mostly rages) and the Humour of living in great, populous and consequently unhealthy Townes

for the particular sensitivity of the Englishman's nerves. Progress has eroded away our toughness, and replaced it with the kind of sympathetic fellow-feeling necessary for complex social interactions, more spiritual forms of Christianity, cheek-by-jowl city life and the appreciation of exquisite food and art.

This was something new. It was quite different from the melancholia that had affected (and had been affected by) the scholars and brooding poets of the seventeenth century. This was a disease of society itself. It was not a symptom of one's alienation from society, but proof of one's achievement of its highest refinements. Within a decade the English novel had been invented, and from it the English learned this new way to be mad.

One theory linked the rise of English sensibility with the demise of absolutism and a perceived loss of social cohesion. In the old world, so it goes, the sovereign holds society together by sheer force. In an emerging democracy, society has to hold itself together by means of millions of mutual bonds of sympathy and care between priest and flock, landowner and peasant, industrialist and worker, businessman and businessman, neighbour and neighbour. These sensibilities must be reinforced and heightened to sustain – or perhaps re-forge – such bonds in the absence of the old, rigid order of things. The theory does not explain how, in the early eighteenth century, sensibility also arose in countries whose political and social histories were as different as France and the German-speaking states.

Sensibility is not a malady affecting the English as a whole. Cheyne observes that it affects those city-dwellers who work in sedentary jobs: what we would later call the middle classes. The capitalism of the late seventeenth century had created an army of bureaucrats that would mushroom as the industrial revolution got underway: accountants and clerks, buyers and salesmen, stockjobbers and brokers, regulators and record-keepers, journalists, and thousands of small-businessmen who found capital accruing to them more easily than it had to previous generations thanks to a staggering influx of wealth from overseas. This group had disposable income but, because it grew rapidly, lacked a clear social identity. In 1600 personal identity was defined for most people by a fixed place in the social order. This in turn was largely defined by birth. By 1700 this was no longer precisely the case. Parents' wealth and status remained, as today, an excellent predictor of the wealth and status of their children but we find an additional anxiety about defining and expressing one's place in society.

There was another symptom of this malady. In 1600 the possessions of even a comfortably-off craftsman might be counted on his fingers and toes, but by 1700 the objects the better sort of home contained had begun to multiply significantly. The identity of the new middle class was hedged-in by *things*; a consumer society was being born. The search for that identity was provided with a road map by publications such as Addison and Steele's *Spectator* that set a common benchmark of taste not only in interior decoration and reading matter but also in manners, feeling, politics and even spirituality. It was in this context that the code of sensibility was first compiled. Sensibility is a code of civilised, humanitarian fellow-feeling; a reaction against a perceived hardness required by the previous age. The follower of sensibility was refined, delicate, susceptible to upset, to tears or fainting in the presence of the slightest agitation. Death or suffering in another caused sympathetic resonances in the observer, and the more cultivated the observer the more strongly they would be felt. Like the pale skin of the aristocrat that spoke of the luxury of idleness, this delicacy was cultivated by those who did not work, or who wished to appear as if they did not. It was also, of course, more readily accepted in women, who were already considered weak, fair, gentle, soft, sociable and impressionable. Middle-class men, many of whom worked in the sometimes harsh worlds of trade or industry, had their own rituals of hardness. Yet inasmuch as they aspired to appear aristocratic, some such men also aspired towards sensibility. Gould and Pyle's *Anomalies and Curiosities of Medicine* (1896) contains a wonderful, if often spurious, collection of eighteenth-century nervous disorders, including the French lady possessed of such a delicate constitution that she fainted away at the sight of a boiled lobster. Such states lurk on the borderline between the sensitive, over-cultivated, accomplished, polished, but wholly artificial Baroque urbanite – which was fashionable – and actual insanity, which remained stigmatised. Many such states we would today diagnose as phobias or stress-related illnesses. Freud would have called them 'neuroses' and treated them by bringing their supposed subconscious causes to the surface, whereas today they are largely managed pharmaceutically. Where, precisely, the line between the two is drawn has as much to do with the patient's social and economic position as with actual symptoms. The eccentric aristocrat may indulge in far more exotic states of mind than the worker can afford. Those anxious middle classes for whom the aristocrat was a bellwether had to carefully negotiate a position somewhere between the two.

All this sensibility required education, and it was provided not only by magazines like the *Spectator* but also novels. A generation learned how to pour out its soul in letters from works like Richardson's *Pamela* (1740), Rousseau's *Julie, ou la nouvelle Héloïse* (1761) and Julie de Lespinasse's *Lettres* published in 1809. Later they learned the more intensely private practice of confiding to a diary from Mme de Staël's *Journal de mon coeur* (1785), Lavater's *Diary of an Observer of Himself* (c. 1773) and a slew of works, often borderline-fictional, throughout the nineteenth century. They also learned from depictions of sensitive characters in novels, especially male characters like Harley in Mackenzie's *The Man of Feeling* (1771) who cries at the sight of a pathetic inmate of Bedlam, or at a more extreme peak, Goethe's *The Sorrows of Young Werther* (1774), whose end caused a commotion of copycat suicides among the pale young men of northern Europe. No sooner had the sentimental novel emerged than it was satirised by the likes of Fielding (*Shamela*, 1741), Sterne (*A Sentimental Journey*, 1768) and, much later, Austen (*Sense and Sensibility*, 1811), although in many cases works we read as satirical today seem to originally have been enjoyed with little or no irony. Austen's late date – three generations after Fielding – hints at the longevity of sensibility in England. It was a phenomenon more deeply felt than terms like 'cult' or 'fashion' suggest.

The sentimental novel is contemporaneous with those morbid, brooding lyrics associated with the 'Graveyard Poets' such as Thomas Grey, who in 1751 wrote his 'Elegy Written in a Country Churchyard':

Perhaps in this neglected spot is laid
Some heart once pregnant with celestial fire;
Hands, that the rod of empire might have sway'd,
Or waked to ecstasy the living lyre:

Grey, said the troubled Christopher Smart, 'walks as if he had fouled his small-clothes and looks as if he smelt it', but this poetry of poised melancholy found an eager audience in the middle of the eighteenth century. Indeed, many of the preoccupations of the Romantic poets of a later generation are prefigured in the middle-brow 'magazine poetry' of this time, poetry published by people like Addison and Steele, their fingers on the pulse of middle-class anxieties and aspirations. The sentimentality, the desire to flee the harshness of the city for the countryside, and the emphasis on simple and even rustic style over the baroque virtuosity of Pope and his contemporaries are all already present there. Coleridge and Wordsworth were to put all this on a rather different philosophical footing, but their poetry does not spring from nowhere.

Smart's own relationship with mental illness is another story, later ennobled by Robert Browning in his poem 'Parleyings With Christopher Smart', where

> Smart, solely of such songmen, pierced the screen
> 'Twixt thing and word, lit language straight from soul,–

and was thus struck by genius at the moment madness took hold of him. The two are inseparable, for his madness gives him insight into the ineffable. In modern discussions Smart's madness is often described as a religious mania, a kind of obsessive devotional mysticism that eclipsed everything else in his life. Other causes have been put forward. Some have noted that he was committed to an asylum by his family during a financial dispute, and have speculated that he was sane enough when he entered it. Others have pointed to the alcoholism of his youth, which was combined with a general physical frailty.

German-language culture around the 1770s saw a comparable development that would be widely influential, and became known as *Sturm und Drang*, 'storm and stress'. Some prose works of Goethe and the dramas of Schiller fall into this style. Haydn, Mozart, Carl Philipp Emanuel Bach and Gluck are commonly said to have adopted this style as a phase; it explains, at least on one account, the minor-key, brooding and dissonant works like Haydn's Symphony No 44 and, a little later, Mozart's *Don Giovanni*. Today we call this period Classical, reserving the term Romantic for those born in the magical 1770s, the decade of the 'Romantic generation'. Yet the latter half of the eighteenth century is better seen as gently moving away from the formal purity of Classicism proper towards looser, more experimental practices that would be brought fully into the open by, for example,

Beethoven. It represents the development of 'sensibility' from a polite, social, humane quality cultivated for the improvement of the common life into something darker and more individualistic – more destructive and at the same time more creative. The emotions of 'sensibility' had been reduced to a set of conventions, and Romanticism was set to reject these, while embracing a search for intensity and a move from social cohesion to individual genius. In 1791, while Coleridge and Wordsworth were still university students, Mozart finally composed for the glass harmonica, and died at the end of that year.

The precursor of the glass harmonica was a table holding a number of tuned wine glasses. You can make your own, and in fact there is a simple experiment you can try with just two empty wine glasses – the sort with stems, and the thinner the better (fine crystal, should you have some to hand, is the best). Place them close together on a table, but not touching. Dip one finger in some water and rub it around the rim of one glass to produce a strong, clear note. Be careful not to make it ring too loudly to avoid shattering the glass. While the note is sounding, suddenly stop it by placing your whole hand gently around the goblet. If you listen carefully, you should continue to hear the note, very faintly, like a ghostly echo. It is coming from the other glass, as you can verify by stopping it with your hand. This is the phenomenon known as sympathetic resonance. If you have trouble hearing it, put a light wire, straw or cocktail stick across the top of the second glass; even if you don't hear the pitch, you will see the vibrations causing the object to move.

These subtle physical resonances inspired some to wonder whether there was not a human equivalent that worked (in the sane) to distinguish right from wrong. Might not a sympathy of this sort be another of the opposites of madness? This idea resonated (and later came into conflict) with the early eighteenth-century philosophy of the rationalists, led by Leibniz and Wolff and ubiquitous in Western Europe. To them it seemed it should be possible to deduce all the true principles of moral action just as a geometer deduces the properties of a triangle. At the end of the century, this thought still underpinned Erskine's argument at the trial of Hadfield: that one finds the right and wrong in a situation by the use of reason alone, and that if this faculty is impaired it will lead to false judgements for which that person may not be entirely blameworthy. This might remind us of Aristotle: after all, we do not hold animals morally culpable for their misdeeds, since they lack rationality, and to a lesser extent the same applies to young children. Aristotle was out of vogue in the eighteenth century, redolent as he was of dusty university schoolmen still inflicting a mediæval curriculum on their charges. But by the time Erskine made rationalism the basis of his argument the notion that reason was the key to morality had become unfashionable. In the middle of the century a new idea had emerged from a somewhat older tradition: the notion of a 'sixth sense', sitting outside of rationality, that guided moral judgements.

In part this was a response to the very real practical difficulties of deriving satisfactory moral laws or guidelines from reason alone. In part, too, it arose because of a general decline in the popularity of rationalism. Christians had already begun to develop spiritual practices derived from personal experience that became increasingly popular as the century wore on. In Germany there was Pietism, which influenced Puritanism and Methodism in the English-speaking world. This turn to individual, personal religious experience touched the field of moral philosophy in many places, perhaps most famously in Adam Smith's *Theory of Moral Sentiments* (1759). Much earlier, in 1699, the Earl of Shaftesbury had proposed a 'moral sense' that perceives right and wrong just as the sense of smell perceives odours. The analogy is appealing: it makes morality an objective matter and dispels any possibility of moral judgements being merely relative. Yet Shaftesbury thought the same could be applied to 'taste in art'. No need to confuse matters with subjectivity: it was just a matter of the proper response to an objective stimulus. Understanding it was just a question of understanding the qualities of the stimulus that gave rise to the required sensations. The idea was developed by Francis Hutcheson in *An Essay on the Nature and Conduct of the Passions and Affections, with Illustrations on the Moral Sense* (1742). When I observe someone helping a stranger, the perception I receive literally includes the moral goodness of the act, just as it includes the colours, sounds and smells that the other senses apprehend. In the same way, as Hutcheson had earlier argued (*An Inquiry into the Original of Our Ideas of Beauty and Virtue*, 1726), when I hear Mozart's *Adagio for Glass Harmonica* my perception includes the formal beauty of the music as well as its mere sound. This 'sixth sense' is a literal sensing of a moral fact just as sight represents a literal sensing of a fact about light and colour. For this to work, it has to be an instantaneous process that bypasses logical and rational thought processes: the slow-witted village 'natural' sees a red ball in the same way that I do even if he cannot reason from that to predictions about its behaviour when thrown. I know that an act of stealing is wrong in the same way that I know

In 1812 Millman Street was home to John Bellingham, who had been wrongly imprisoned for five years in Russia over a shipping insurance scandal. He tried to win compensation from the British government but got nowhere. So he waited in the lobby of the House of Commons until the Prime Minister, Spencer Perceval, appeared, and he shot him dead. Was he insane? The judge thought not, and he was hanged a week later.

that a flame is hot. Erskine's argument swims against this naturalising stream, arguing that Hadfield cannot be held responsible for his actions because of an impairment not of his sensory faculties but of his rational one, embodied in his severed 'nerves'.

This debate made central a question that is now not often asked: can moral truths be scientifically discovered? Since observations made by the other senses were held to be the foundation of science, the 'sixth sense' theory held out as much hope in this area as the rationalist one it sought to supplant. Yet it also brought with it the rather unsettling thought that our moral sense might be merely subjective and relative. In the hands of the arch-sceptic David Hume, for example, the moral sense was transformed into a mere pleasant sort of feeling engendered by good deeds and a corresponding distaste for evil. In fact, his theory owed more than a little to the Renaissance ideas about sympathetic magic that would influence Mesmer: I feel happy when I see a drowning man rescued because I *sympathise* with the man. The verb 'to sympathise' first appears in English in the 1570s in connection with Paracelsian medicine, which relies on the harmonious balance of the microcosm of the body with the macrocosm of the universe, and thus on those practices involving action at a distance that appear most superstitious to us today. Similarly, Hume's moral sense is aroused by a literal transfer of vibration, the way a glass resonates sympathetically when one nearby is rubbed. It is even aroused, he says, when we witness the mere pantomime of a drowning man rescued at the theatre, because moral value is no longer something mysterious in the event conveyed to us (as colour is conveyed to us through the eyes by the medium of light) but something that is in us – a string waiting to be plucked or bowed. Morality becomes a kind of harmony; even Hume's scepticism does not transcend the worldview he has inherited from the Renaissance. This unspoken, Cosmic-Platonic-Hermetic-Pythagorean worldview continued to fascinate Arthur Machen: '*Quod superius est sicut quod inferius* ("that which is above is as that which is below"), as the Smaragdine Tablet of Hermes Trismegistus testifies'. For Adam Smith, too, in his *Theory of Moral Sentiments* (1759) the moral sentiments are theatrical, and social life is a world of greasepaint and limelight in which each of us performs on our own individual stage, and is offstage only when alone. This is society as spectacle, in which each moral action is a potential performance, and each individual is always open to the gaze of all.

Hume's theory of moral sense leads to obvious concerns about those for whom the feelings seem to be reversed: for whom evil is pleasant and good is not. Are such people unfortunate enough to be evil by nature, or do they just have different preferences from us? This has ever been the hazard of reducing ethics to aesthetics. *De gustibus non disputandem:* if you like celery and I do not, there is little you can say to convince me to alter my taste and *vice versa*, and little reason why we would care to do so – you can eat celery and I can avoid it. We cannot afford to be so inclusive about morality. Hence, we continue to pathologise those who make what we think are bad moral choices, especially in cases where they show no sign of understanding that the choice was bad. And so James Hadfield, whose attempt on the king's life was not such a good choice, was packed off to Bethlem Hospital in Moorfields. The site of the hospital is now covered with an imposing terrace of Victorian offices between London Wall and Finsbury Circus.

It is a startling fact that at the beginning of the eighteenth century, Bethlem Hospital – Bedlam, as it was popularly known – held a hundred or so inmates who were the only people forcibly incarcerated due to madness in the whole country. The asylum was a product of eighteenth century entrepreneurship, an opportunity for profit that created a 'trade in lunacy'. This was a case of the supply-side expansion of a market inflating demand that had previously hardly existed. Estimates of ten thousand under lock and key in 1800 (when the population had less than trebled) and a hundred thousand by 1900 are widely cited; this was a thousand-fold increase compared with a less-than-tenfold rise in population. A boom industry, by any standards. The increasing power and scope of medicine as a discipline was a major factor: Ian Hacking describes the late eighteenth century as 'one of the great periods of imperial expansion' of medicine, implying a scramble to acquire territory from other disciplines. Another factor was the way private asylums were incentivised to retain their clients, not to cure them, some not asking too many questions about new business even if it issued from the desire to spirit away an inconvenient wife or elderly relative rather than any genuine disorder.

At the same time, as a counter-balance to rapidly proliferating numbers of inmates, asylums were coming to be seen as places of treatment rather than permanent residences for those whom society did not want. In the early nineteenth century, the surgeon Robert Gardiner Hill attempted to abolish mechanical restraint at Lincoln Asylum; his goal was

> Moral treatment with a view to induce habits of… self-control and cleanliness, which qualities are both essential to recovery, and yet cannot possibly be attained unto by a patient under restraint.

This represents a new theory of mental illness that made it explicitly a matter of morality, not a physical dysfunction. It flirts with a relativistic position that madness itself is a mere construction of culture. This is the danger of detaching the *psyche* from the physical body, and most of the trend was in the opposite direction despite the superficially humane aspects of Hill's regime.

Esquirol, head physician at Salpêtrière in the 1810s and 1820s, presided over the medicalisation of madness in France. He argued publicly with an English physician called Burrows over whether England or France had the worst suicide statistics and, hence, which race or environment was most predisposed to madness. Both men were organicists, convinced that any form of apparent mental illness is a symptom of some physical disease of an organ in the body. This view was quite opposed to the moralising strand evident in Robert Gardiner Hill, and afforded asylums the licence to experiment with all manner of physical and medical treatments. Bloodletting with leeches, for example, 'was never so widely employed as in France between 1815 and 1835' in attempts to cure various illnesses, according to Hacking, who attributes this curious statistic to the fact that medical men of this period had come of age during the Napoleonic wars in which diseases such as typhus and phlebitis – then treated by bloodletting – were a serious problem: the 'enthusiasm for "irritation" and "inflammation" as key medical concepts arose during the war years'.

Alongside novel treatments, the physicians at Salpêtrière were developing an ambitious theory of the mind that sought to move away from speculation or impractical scepticism and base itself on careful measurements and observation of physical facts. The painter Théodore Géricault played a part in its development, but it was not his first collaboration with the medical world. At some point in 1817 he got acquainted with the staff at the Hôpital Beaujon, a fine pre-Revolutionary building that stood next to his studio on the Rue du Faubourg Saint Honoré, then on the outskirts of Paris. The hospital had originally been surrounded by a kind of artificial bucolic environment, with English gardens, a dairy and other features deemed calming to its tenants. After its owner's death the land had been parcelled up and partly transformed into commercial pleasure gardens; in the year Géricault met his neighbours, a new attraction had just been unveiled, a huge roller-coaster-like contraption called The Mountains of Paris. Géricault wished to study anatomy, and he did so by making drawings of patients, corpses and body parts at the hospital. This was a fairly traditional part of an artist's training, although he seems to have gone about it with somewhat unusual seriousness. When Géricault sought to create his first large-scale canvas he cast about for contemporary subjects. In the end he settled on the most scandalous and horrifying story of recent years: the wreck in 1810 of the frigate Méduse off the coast of Senegal and the ordeal undergone by its survivors. A hundred and fifty men took to a large, makeshift raft as the Méduse sank, but were unable to secure provisions. That same night saw the first murders and suicides. The raft was more than two weeks adrift before it was found, the remaining fifteen survivors having systematically murdered the rest and, in some cases, resorted to cannibalism. It was a national scandal, since the captaincy of the Méduse had been given to the Viscount de Chaumareys more for his loyalty to Louis XVIII than for his experience at sea.

Géricault's *The Raft of the Medusa* is now one of the most celebrated works of nineteenth-century painting. He threw all he had learned at Beaujon into his rendering of the tangle of distressed bodies that makes up its bulk. Its heroic composition – a figure at the top silhouetted against towering seas – is severely undercut by the grim carpet of sprawling corpses on which it is based. The painting was exhibited at the Salon Carré in 1819 and met with instant success. Géricault was praised by the Academie; accounts that focus on his later troubles sometimes omit this fact, emphasising its shocking subject-matter. Its Republican subtext may have alienated some, but by the time it went on display the political affair was over and virtually all agreed that the policy of naval appointments had been a mistake. And, although the painting is remarkable for its vast size and impressiveness, it used technical resources and even themes that were quite conventional by that time. The painting was therefore more comforting a presence than it seems to be today, for by borrowing the language of political and historical painting it recovered something heroic from a shameful national tragedy.

It was not, however, sufficiently comforting to be purchased by the court of Louis XVIII, as Géricault had hoped. The production of such a demanding work on such a scale, without commission, had placed considerable physical, emotional and financial stress on the artist. His failure to find a buyer, and continued grizzling from monarchist critics about the politics of the painting, drove him into a decline. Géricault's behaviour became self-destructive and he eventually sought help at Salpêtrière, where a certain Dr Georget is said to have treated him using the latest scientific advances in the field of mental illness. Géricault, impoverished, made ten paintings of inmates of the hospital as payment in kind.

Georget, however, was not an ordinary doctor and the paintings were not ordinary paintings. Like his superior, Esquirol, Georget was a student of the celebrated Franz Joseph Gall. All three pursued a psychology that was robustly anti-metaphysical: the 'moral sentiments' and other higher functions were not seated in some separate mental dimension, as Enlightenment thinkers like Hutcheson and Adam Smith had thought, but in organs of the body, specifically the brain. They were turning their backs on fuzzy, introspective psychology towards something they hoped would be open to objective discovery by dissection. They were, in other words, phrenologists.

Phrenology located what had once been spiritual matters – moral and aesthetic judgement, what we today call mental illnesses, and perhaps even religious experience – in physical properties of the brain. Since these matters are complex, so must the brain be: it must be composed of parts, each responsible for a different function and capable of its own pathologies. Since the function of the cranium is to contain the brain, some of the grosser features of the brain can be read off from the shape of the head. The idea, they believed, was not implausible: the size of an organ is correlated with its capacity for work, so a big heart pumps blood more powerfully, large lungs can take up oxygen more quickly, and so on. And just as something like lung function (in modern terms) rests on both genetic inheritance and conditioning, so the phrenologists believed that we owed our mental faculties to the inherited size and shape of our brains as well as environmental factors. The paintings Géricault made for Dr Georget were not conventional portraits but phrenological 'models', supposed to present the outward appearance of the 'type' of a kleptomaniac or hysteric, say, as an aid to diagnosis. Their subjects are anonymous; more specifically, their subjects are not really people at all but dispositions of bodies that disclose clues to the trained clinician.

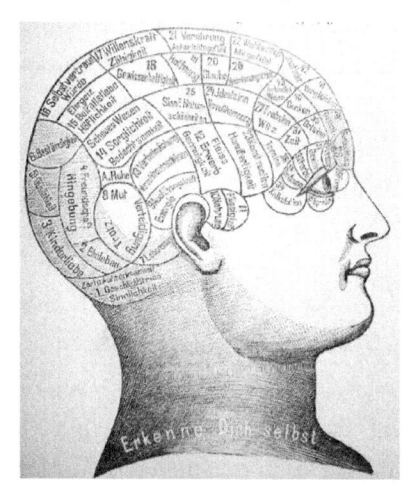

One phrenologist lived at 45 Guilford Street. Forbes Benignus Winslow came from a family in a financially parlous state thanks to their having been on the wrong side of the American War of Independence. It is said that he paid for his medical education by moonlighting as a House of Commons reporter for The Times. He wrote numerous works on the relationship between madness and the law. *The Plea of Insanity in Criminal Cases* (1843) called for a wider definition of 'insanity', raising as an example the possibility of a person's committing a crime while sleepwalking. Some of his opinions were controversial. In 1854 he testified as an expert witness in the case of one Mary Brough, who had slit the throats of six of her own children. His opinion was that 'the act itself bears insanity stamped on its very face', little further evidence being required. Yet John Charles Bucknill, a fellow expert in the legal status of insanity writing later that year, blasted Winslow for providing an apology for a woman who had acted 'vindictively', murdering her children as an act of revenge against her husband. Such tragic events still do very occasionally occur; since 1948 psychoanalysts have referred to such murderers as suffering from the 'Medea Complex' and their legal status is still problematic.

As a medical psychologist Winslow was strongly influenced by phrenology, especially its organicism: he published *The Softening of the Brain from Anxiety* and hoped his crowning achievement would be a volume entitled *On the Softening of the Brain*, a work he died before completing. (His son, who followed his father into medicine, founded a hospital in his honour and went on to seize fifteen minutes of fame by claiming to have identified Jack the Ripper by means of a psychological profile so detailed that it frightened the culprit into hiding. The authorities found his efforts tiresomely unhelpful.) Winslow's *magnum opus* remains *On Obscure Diseases of the Brain and Disorders of the Mind* (1860). In it he provides a magisterial and moving account of his life's work:

> Like the historian and antiquarian wandering with a sad heart over ground made classical and memorable in the story of great men, and in the annals of heroic deeds, surveying with painful interest the crumbling ruins of ancient temples, viewing with subdued emotion the almost extinguished remains of proud imperial cities, consecrated by the genius of men renowned in the world's history as statesmen, scholars, artists, philosophers, and poets, so it is the duty of the mental physician to wander through the sad ruins of still greater temples than any that were in ancient days raised to the honour of an unseen Deity. It is his distressing province to witness great and good intellects, proud, elevated understandings, levelled to the earth, crumbling like dust in the balance, under the dire influence of disease.

Many functions were ascribed to the physical characteristics of the brain – as many as today are considered genetic – including sexuality, propensity to violence, gregariousness and obedience to authority. Another was musical talent. If you believe that this is a trait inherited at birth, you owe a great deal of this belief to the phrenologists who first proposed a plausible mechanism for it. Later, at the turn of the twentieth century, such mechanisms would come to seem less important: the behaviourism of John B. Watson would emphasise measurable, external events over internal mental states or their supposed causes. In this spirit, in 1919, Carl Seashore produced a set of four phonograph disks designed to measure musical talent by testing subjects' abilities to discriminate pitch, loudness, rhythm, timbre and consonance. He hoped that young people interested in pursuing a musical career could be put through these tests as a kind of coarse filter. Later critics pointed out that tests like these will always embody a pre-analytical definition of what counts as musical talent and, indeed, what is important in music. The abilities tested by Seashore were precisely those that modernist composers of the time were concerned to liberate from traditional practices. Abilities such as memory, manual dexterity, attention to detail or stage presence are conspicuous by their absence. It points to a deeper question: can we know 'what music is' or 'what musical ability is' at all?

For the phrenologists the problem was more immediate: they were unable to make any connection between brains and minds by means of dissection or other biological methods. Since the phrenologists lacked the technological means to test their own claims directly, they resorted to a broadly statistical approach. Unfortunately they often mangled and cherry-picked their data, or found in the skulls they inspected whatever they expected to find based on what they already knew about their owners, whether a lag in the local prison or the child of a monarch. They were probably unwitting victims of the subconscious desire to confirm one's prejudices, rather than perpetrators of cynical deception, although undoubtedly there were also sideshow barkers who adopted phrenology as an easy moneyspinner, and it was this sort of thing, not a rejection of their general project, that led to the field being discredited. Today it is fashionable for historians to recuperate phrenology, to their readers' imagined surprise: but the question remains whether the phrenologists were in important ways right or whether some areas of modern science in fact remain enthralled by much the same fallacies.

Another physician and insanity specialist, John Haslam, spent much of his career as apothecary at Bethlem Hospital. His *Observations on Madness and Melancholy* (1809) contains case study after case study of inmates with a wide variety of psychological disorders. He opens up each of their heads after death and faithfully catalogues the size and quality of the grey matter, the amount of fluid, etc., but can make no real sense of it all, and seems to sit there staring at its mysterious workings, baffled and fascinated, like a child that has prised open a laptop; or like the distraught young doctor in Arthur Machen's 'The Inmost Light', who is convinced that Dr Black's wife, the subject of his autopsy, possesses the brain of a devil.

Nevertheless, Haslam's book was innovative in arguing that no single, general definition of the term 'mad' is to be sought. The word simply covers a number of different sorts of illness. In the broadest division, he said, we think of it in terms of 'mania' and 'melancholia'. The latter is familiar to us today and something akin to depression, while the former covers a wide range of symptoms including delusion and violence. As to the origins of mania, Haslam disagrees with his Scottish colleague Dr John Ferriar:

> In mania he conceives 'false perception, and consequently confusion of ideas, to be a leading circumstance'. The latter, he supposes to consist 'in intensity of idea, which is a contrary state to false perception'. From the observations I have been able to make respecting mania, I have by no means been led to conclude, that false perception, is a leading circumstance in this disorder, and still less, that confusion of ideas must be the necessary consequence of false perception.

Ferriar would later seek to explain away reports of ghosts and other supernatural sightings by the same device: his *Essay Towards a Theory of Apparitions* (1813) argues that false perceptions lie at the root of such phenomena. Thomas Erskine's defence of insanity contained the idea that strange beliefs, behaviours and experiences are the products of erroneous beliefs. Here is a similar notion: that mistakes of perception lie at the roots of the psychologically abnormal. One of Haslam's *Observations* is of an industrious lunatic who amasses capital from basket-weaving, exploiting the other lunatics, and thus hopes to secure his future, but loses his fortune in gaming with a mad soldier, who immediately discharges himself from Bedlam, having done rather well from his brief stay. The penniless lunatic starts to build his business up again, but by then a new inmate has set himself up as a serious commercial rival: a certain Mr Hadfield.

Around the corner from Haslam was a mansion, Queen Square House, built in 1777; today it is gone and the site is occupied by the brutalist concrete of the Institute of Neurology. Eleven years before Hadfield took a shot at him, King George III was brought here after suffering a severe attack of – well, nobody knows. Among modern historians the most common hypothesis is that the king suffered from an acute intermittent porphyria, a physical illness that can produce neurological symptoms. Recently, however, researchers have begun to question this diagnosis, with Peters and Wilkinson claiming that the original proposers of the porphyry hypothesis believed that mental illnesses were

John Haslam lived at 56 Lamb's Conduit Street (the modern number 59) and died there in 1844. He wrote of one inmate of Bethlem: 'R. B. a man, 64 years of age, was admitted into the hospital, September 2, 1797. He had then been disordered three months occasioned by drinking spirituous liquors to excess.' He believed that he had discovered longitude; he believed that he was related to Anacreon, the ancient Greek poet with a reputation for bacchanalian and amatory lyrics ('Lord [Dionysus], with whom Eros the subduer and the blue-eyed Nymphai, and radiant Aphrodite play, as you haunt the lofty mountain peaks'). He lived another three months.

primarily caused by physical diseases, and their diagnosis of George III formed part of a wider agenda to promote controversial views about past, contemporary and future methods in psychiatry.

Controversies about the true nature of mental illness and, more profoundly, the mind's relation to the physical body continue.

King George III suffered his first attack in 1765. A bout in 1788-89 seems to have been more severe, and he was delivered into the care of Francis Willis, a clergyman-turned-physician who claimed to be able to cure him in a matter of months. 'Care' is undoubtedly the wrong word: without any idea of the physical aetiology of the illness, Willis believed the best way to get rid of the king's madness was by shouting at it and otherwise to 'make himself formidable – to inspire awe'. George's treatment consisted of cold baths, severe restraint, beatings, starvation, isolation and procedures that were certainly unpleasant but could find no purchase on his illness. The treatment was observed by a scandalised Countess Harcourt, and as word of it spread through this society of highly-attuned sensibilities so did sympathy for him. It made the treatment of the insane a topic of general conversation. This amplified an already-rising clamour of complaints against the unscientific and inhumane practices of the asylum proprietors that would transform them utterly; a figure like Robert Gardiner Hill, attempting to do away with the practices favoured by the likes of Willis, is emblematic of this transition. If insanity could strike a king, many thought, it could strike anyone; it was no longer something that happened only to other people, mostly the poor and dispossessed whom a previous generation had found so diverting to observe at Bethlem Hospital. The boundary between sanity and madness had grown thinner.

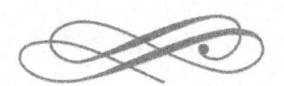

In a story by Arthur Machen called 'N', we are not sure if the mad have not in fact looked into another world. Three antiquarians sit around the fire sipping punch and recalling a part of London with an odd atmosphere to it, which may be connected to the presence of a private asylum:

> some very unpleasant stories got about; I'm not sure if the doctor didn't get mixed up in a lawsuit over a gentleman, of good family, I believe, who had

The Institute of Neurology looms in front of Queen Charlotte. Her husband, King George III, was 'treated' on the site.

been shut up in Himalaya House by his relations for years, and as sensible as you or me all the time. And then there was that young fellow that managed to escape… he contrived to climb out or creep out somehow or other… and walked as quietly as you please up the road, and took lodgings close by here, in that row of old red-brick houses… of course, the doctor's men were after him directly and making inquiries in all directions, but Mrs Wilson never thought for a moment that this quiet young lodger of hers was the missing madman… It was when she was clearing away his tea, he suddenly spoke up, and says: "What I like about these apartments of yours, Mrs Wilson, is the amazing view you have from your windows." …And then, it seems, he began to talk the most outrageous nonsense about golden and silver and purple flowers, and the bubbling well, and the walk that went under the trees right into the wood, and the fairy house on the hill… the doctor's men took the young fellow back.

Other witnesses emerge, and other events transpire, which suggest that the young lodger is not the only one to be vouchsafed such visions. These are reminiscent of certain episodes from Winslow's *On Obscure Diseases of the Brain and Mind*.

Happily, there are many cases of insanity, even in the incipient stage, where the mind is intensely abstracted and pre-occupied in the contemplation of the most glowing, richly poetical, fanciful, and joyous imagery. The morbid imagination exalts its possessor into the purest and most elevated ethereal regions… he is an angelic being, enjoying all the rapturous pleasures and ecstatic bliss of the redeemed, in a brighter and a purer state of existence. I have occasionally seen such patients return to the dull, and often humble realities of sane life; in other words, restored to the possession of reason, and (comparing their normal with their abnormal condition of mind) have been disposed to ask the question, which was the happier state of the two?

In the conclusion to his *Enquiry Concerning Human Understanding* (1748), David Hume observed that philosophy, especially when it leads to extremes of scepticism as it had for him, borders on a kind of madness. His cure was to go out into society and embrace again the quotidian aspects of life:

> Most fortunately it happens, that since reason is incapable of dispelling these clouds, nature herself suffices to that purpose, and cures me of this philosophical melancholy and delirium, either by relaxing this bent of mind, or by some avocation, and lively impression of my senses, which obliterate all these chimeras. I dine, I play a game of backgammon, I converse, and am merry with my friends; and when after three or four hours' amusement, I would return to these speculations, they appear so cold, and strained, and ridiculous, that I cannot find in my heart to enter into them any farther.

Hume remained a man of the Enlightenment despite having demolished so many of its central tenets. He rejected the kind of delirium in which effect might not follow cause, the future may radically differ from the past and those things we firmly believe in may not exist at all. For him it was a powerful device of thought to be overcome; reality was dinner, backgammon and good company. But, restored to the possession of reason, was Hume disposed to ask the question, which was the happier state? In another of Winslow's case studies, a drowning man survives and describes his near-death visions:

> They were the most delightful and ecstatic I have ever experienced. I was transported to a perfect paradise, and witnessed scenes that my imagination never had, in its most active condition, depicted to my mind. I wandered in company with angelic spirits through the most lovely citron and orange groves, 'roseate bowers, celestial palms, and ever-blooming flowers' [a quotation from Pope's 'Eloisa to Abelard'], basking in an atmosphere redolent of the most delicious perfumes. I heard the most exquisite music proceeding from melodious voices and well-tuned instruments.

In the eighteenth century a new manner of music-making emerged in Germany: the *empfindsamer Stil*, the 'highly sensitive style'. Critics compared it to oratory, designed not merely to convey information but to stir the emotions of its listeners, causing a sympathetic response of agitation, sorrow, happiness and so on in its audience. Although different musical qualities had been associated with mental states in the baroque music of the previous century, this was a new and thoroughgoing aesthetic of sensibility, and audiences, anxious to parade their finely-tuned sensibilities, were highly appreciative of it. It is with the *empfindsamer Stil* that we find audiences begin to be moved to tears by purely instrumental music. It is also here that we first see widespread claims that music is language-like. *Empfindsamkeit* – 'sentimentalism' – brought the vogue for those instrumental curiosities whose eerie voices sent shivers down the spine, among them Franklin's glass harmonica. Another is the 'nail violin', a collection of nails driven at different lengths into a wooden sounding-box and agitated with a violin bow. The weird otherworldliness of these sounds, and perhaps their very harshness, were an attraction, particularly for the consumers of the Gothic novel in the audience. The official music of court and concert-hall may have reflected these fashions only palely, and we can imagine that the drawing-rooms of the middle classes occasionally played host to much stranger sonic events.

The musical instrument that would come to represent one of the emblems of Romanticism was not the glass harmonica but the æolian harp. This was another simple folk-instrument, easily constructed by a capable woodworker, and it too possessed an eerie, eldritch quality. It had a property possessed by no other instrument in popular use in the period: it was played not by a human being but by the wind. Samuel Taylor Coleridge wrote a poem named after it. In it the recognisable figure of the lonely bard is subverted: the singer has vanished, leaving only his harp or, perhaps more accurately, the singer has turned into the harp. Nature itself seems to make music on the æolian harp without human interference, and the effect of hearing it in a garden was often described as a kind of enchantment, as if one were in the presence of something supernatural. Since these instruments will sing even in a gentle breeze, perhaps their mystery is enhanced by the way the sound seems to be produced by spontaneous, sympathetic resonance: like the magic of the Renaissance, a harmony is struck up by mysterious action at a distance thanks to the invisibility of the wind. By the time Géricault was working on his great canvas the gardens of England were filled with æolian harps and Romantic poetry was at the height of its vogue.

For the Romantics, Hume's chimeras appeared to belong to reality and the world of polite society seemed but a construct of artificial trivialities to be leapt over. For them, madness came to be a technology of enlightenment; a sign of its achievement; a marker of genius; a way through the veil. They learned from the French Revolution that to tear away the deception and alienation of the modern world required the rejection of its norms of behaviour and even of belief. Blake and Wordsworth looked to the child before socialisation had spoiled it. Coleridge turned to bottle after bottle of laudanum. Keats and Shelley cultivated sensitivity to a new end, not humanitarian sociality but separateness, a kind of monastic attunement to something drowned out by the trivial chatter of the town.

And, at the same time as the Romantics were seeing madness in a new light, John Haslam was walking from Lamb's Conduit Street to Moorfields each day and also trying to stretch his understanding of the essence of madness. He came to believe that trying to separate out the different mental faculties (including perception) and label one as deficient is largely a waste of time. A cobbler who believes himself an emperor: is this a failing of perception, judgement, memory or all three? Such imponderables led him towards more pragmatic matters, and above all the question of when it is 'justifiable to deprive a human being of his liberty'. Haslam was more concerned with outward manifestations than the nature of things. In this he was inspired by the empiricist psychology of John Locke.

To understand Locke it almost suffices to understand the concept of science he inherited in large part from René Descartes. The French physicist and philosopher had been one of the most celebrated figures in all of Europe by the time of his death in 1650, when Locke himself was only 18. He made enduring contributions to mathematics, especially his synthesis of ideas about analytical geometry, which allowed ancient problems to be attacked with new algebraic methods. He worked tirelessly in physics, especially optics. He is still read today by every new student of philosophy, because he raised most of the questions that philosophy has busied itself over ever since; it is he, not Plato, who is the real founder of philosophical enquiry in the modern sense. Two aspects of his philosophy relate most directly to Locke: his 'mechanism' and the 'method of doubt'. The former seems unsurprising now, although it was quite radical at the time: it is the notion that the whole of nature is a sort of machine that runs according to the way it has been constructed. It is not a moral universe presided over by providence but one that simply does what it does, and the scientist's job is to penetrate into the principles by which it functions. Only human beings are exempted from its terrible inevitability: being possessed of souls, we make choices using our reason, which is a kind of freedom. All other animals, he notoriously said, are mere machines, dead things made to move by the clockwork of nature in the way that a rock is animated by falling from a ledge. Locke was born into a world that was already Cartesian, and that saw the path to mastery as one of learning to work the machine of nature rather than seeking the mysterious correspondences that had seduced the neoplatonist magicians of the previous century. The 'method of doubt', too, now feels suspiciously modern. In the opening of his *Meditations* Descartes speaks of a moment of personal crisis in which he realises that everything he thinks he knows, he has actually learned from uncertain sources – from authorities, perhaps, or from his senses, both of which are entirely fallible. He decides that the only way to be sure of anything is to doubt everything, and see whether he can find anything so certain it cannot be doubted. The fixed point he discovers is the famous *cogito ergo sum* – I think, therefore I am – and from this he claims to rebuild the Christian faith, common-sense knowledge and science.

For Locke the method of doubt was compelling but Descartes' efforts at rebuilding looked inadequate: he had not doubted hard enough, especially when it came to establishing the reliability of the senses. Locke's own position is often interpreted by reference to a 'veil of perception', through which we cannot pass. Our minds contain only representations of the world, and these are all we can have knowledge of. We might in reality be completely deceived about how things are. It is not in doubt that something comes through our senses to create the simple ideas in our minds – that something now is hot, or white, or smells of cinnamon – for Locke considers it quite impossible that such ideas can have been invented by a single mind in the absence of external stimulation. Locke does not doubt that the external world exists, but he does doubt that we can be sure we know it as it is. For that, we need to proceed with care, step by step, armed with critical doubt at every turn.

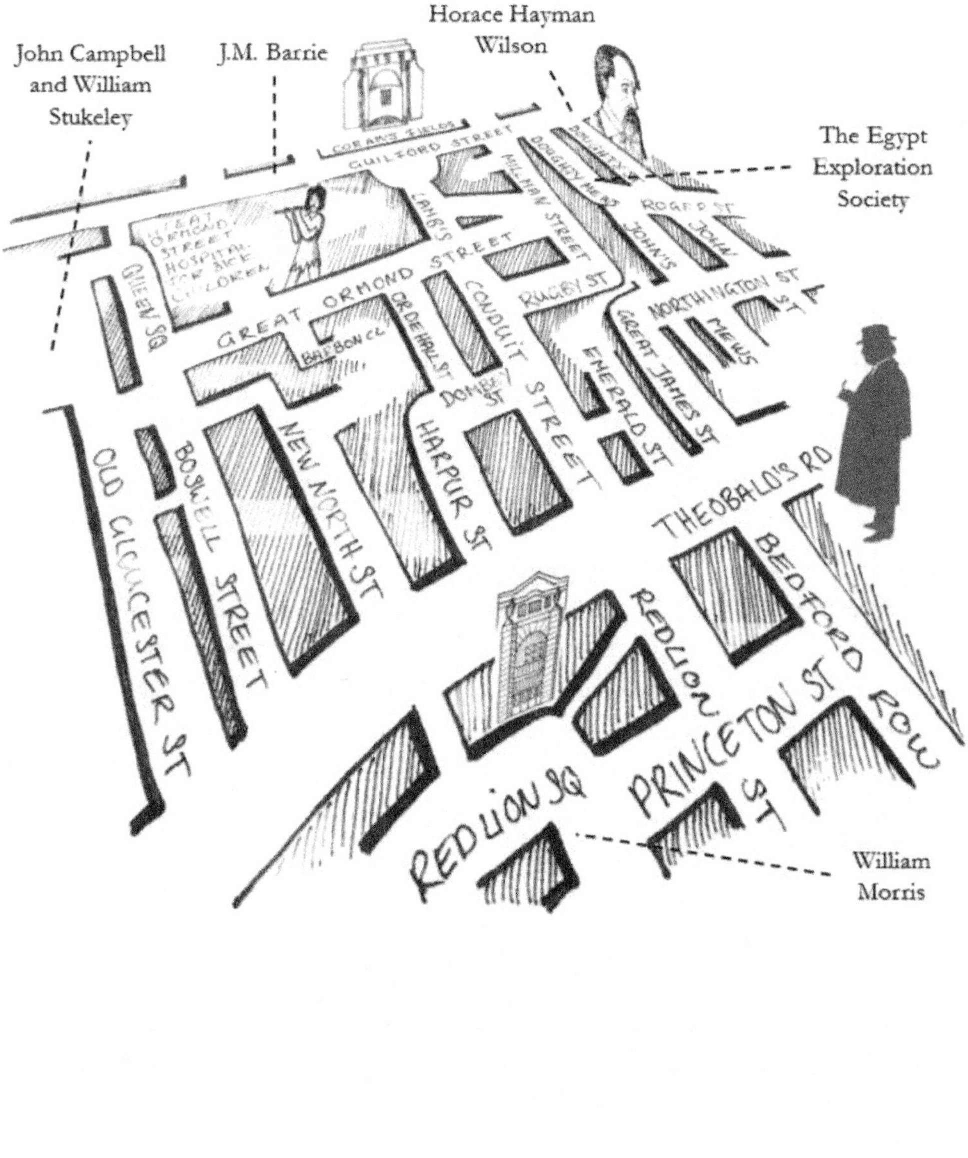
John Campbell and William Stukeley
J.M. Barrie
Horace Hayman Wilson
The Egypt Exploration Society
William Morris
GUILFORD STREET
GREAT ORMOND STREET HOSPITAL FOR SICK CHILDREN
QUEEN SQ
GREAT ORMOND STREET
LAMB'S
MILMAN STREET
DOUGHTY MEWS
JOHN'S
ROGER ST
RUGBY ST
CONDUIT STREET
NORTHINGTON ST
MEWS
GREAT JAMES ST
EMERALD ST
DOMBEY ST
HARPUR ST
NEW NORTH ST
BOSWELL STREET
OLD GLOUCESTER ST
THEOBALD'S RD
BEDFORD ROW
RED LION
PRINCETON ST
RED LION SQ

THE TRIBES OF EUROPE

In 'The Novel of the Black Seal' from *The Three Impostors*, Arthur Machen explicitly connects the ancient Welsh Celts with the myth of fairy-folk. In a later bibliographical note he explains that he took them to be an ancient race of diminutive, dark-skinned people who preceded the people now living in Wales. But his fantasy is this: they still persist, hiding in the hills.

Fairies had been the subject of an extended fascination in the nineteenth century; they had been painted and drawn, appeared in novels, on the stage and above all in verse, and these were not by any means consumed largely by children. The beings Machen describes, however, do not seem much like those of Barrie's Peter Pan. It is hard to be sure how many of the earnest-sounding reports of belief in fairies found in the Victorian and Edwardian periods we should take seriously. Is it possible that such apparently silly beliefs survived in the age of the railway and the telegraph? On inspection some accounts seem to be literary inventions, others fashionable affectation: among the fairytellers we find Christina Rossetti, Robert Browning, Lewis Carroll, John Ruskin, Charles Dickens, Oscar Wilde and William Thackeray. In other cases it appears that the author has attempted a more ethnographic approach such as asking 'local folk' about their beliefs, but one cannot help feeling that they might have often received answers calculated to please or even mock the enquirer. There were certainly some on the mystical fringes who took them seriously, albeit often in reinterpreted form: to the spiritualists they were minor demons; some more mainstream Christians called them 'uncommitted' angels, while among the Theosophists they were the spirits of the elements. The question of whether people 'believed in fairies' is more complex than it first appears.

According to John Rhys, writing in 1901, the fairies of Celtic folklore were 'a swarthy population of short stumpy men occupying the most inaccessible districts of our country' who supplemented their bare subsistence with thieving from humans and improved their stock by the kidnapping and the substitution of changelings:

> The other FAIRIES, when kidnapping, it is true, preferred the blond infants of other people to their own SWARTHY brats

Unlike the diminutive gossamer-winged sprites of Cottingly, these fairies were 'not extravagantly unlike other people in personal appearance', which accords with much that has been written about folk beliefs concerning fairies and similar creatures since. Rhys saw these stories as remnants of clashes arising from long-forgotten migrations of peoples with distinct cultural and racial attributes. It would certainly explain some things: the fairy ring and other signs of occupation perhaps represented sites of encampments, changelings and adult fairies being mistaken for ordinary humans and, indeed, the apparent persistence of belief in something that otherwise seems rather unlikely.

The exhibition of human curiosities reached its peak in the Victorian age, when they were often presented as scientific 'specimens'. These included midgets, pygmies, Eskimos and others who exhibited marked physiological differences from Europeans. When these were in one way or another diminutive they were often referred to as 'fairies', 'elves' or 'dwarves' just as the unusually large were tagged as 'giants'. They were not confined to sideshow tents: they were paraded before aristocrats and featured in high-status exhibitions like those at the Crystal Palace. Parts were specially written for them in theatrical productions; they were inspected by royalty. At its simplest level the freak-show reassures us by showing us what we have in common; it tells us that we are us and they are them, drawing a border around the former by excluding the latter. Yet this is only the crudest level at which it works. The half-supernatural, half-biological language in use and other meaningful aspects of their presentation suggest, by being repeated many times in many places, something is being explored or worked out here.

In 1866 Matthew Arnold, in his capacity as chair of poetry at Oxford, gave a series of four lectures entitled 'On the Study of Celtic Literature'. They were printed in series in the popular monthly *Cornhill Magazine*. He positioned himself at the beginning of a newly-scientific study of race, language and culture, and stated his aim: to demonstrate 'the benefit we may all derive from knowing the Celt and things Celtic more thoroughly' or, as he puts it later,

> What we want is to know the Celt and his genius; not to exalt him or to abase him, but to know him. And for this a disinterested, positive, and constructive criticism is needed.

In Wilhelm von Humboldt – a 'genuine Teuton' – Arnold finds a message of unity in diversity: in spite of the old prejudices he inherited from his father, Humboldt holds the Saxon (as he calls the English) and the Celt as 'our brothers in the great Indo-European family' – disturbingly, in contrast to the 'alien Semitic genius' of the Abrahamic religions. Indeed, Arnold sees the British as a mixed race whose 'genius' must be understood as the compound of those pure elements that merged to form it:

> The Germanic genius has steadiness as its main basis, with commonness and humdrum for its defect, fidelity to nature for its excellence. The Celtic genius, sentiment as its main basis, with love of beauty, charm, and spirituality for its excellence, ineffectualness and self-will for its defect. The Norman genius, talent for affairs as its main basis, with strenuousness and clear rapidity for its excellence, hardness and insolence for its defect. And now to try and trace these in the composite English genius.

For Welsh literature, Arnold leans heavily on the best source available to him, Owen Jones's *Y Myvyrian Archæology*, published in three costly volumes between 1801 and 1807. Among Jones's most important primary sources were the works of Iolo Morgannwg, which are now known to be forgeries. Jones was buried at All-Hallows-On-The Wall, near Moorgate: as Arnold wistfully put it, his tomb is 'turned towards the east, away from the green vale of Clwyd and the mountains of his native Wales', although his grave was later relocated to the London Necropolis. Arnold rails against pretentious translations of Welsh literature that turn it into somewhat proper Victorian, neo-Classical stuff, complete with references to Greek mythology and ritual. In trying to dignify their material and tie the Druidic traditions back to Roman ones, these philologists, he says, create absurd distortions. Arnold wishes to see such things — however well-intentioned they may be — overtaken by real scientific study. His tone is not unlike Erasmus in the early sixteenth century, arguing with traditionalists that the Vulgate needed to be brought up to date with recently-much-improved knowledge of Biblical Hebrew in the West. Arnold wants to 'detect this precious and genuine part in them, and employ it for the elucidation of the Celt's genius and history' — the 'part' in question being the pre-Christian. He and his contemporaries were very concerned with the claim that supposedly 'ancient' Welsh texts were in fact mediæval in date, influenced by the French romance tradition, which would mean that their authentic Welshness would be much diluted. It is this authenticity that Arnold is interested in capturing — this racial and cultural essence — this genius of the people:

> There is evidently mixed here, with the newer legend, a detritus, as the geologists would say, of something far older; and the secret of Wales and its genius is not truly reached until this detritus, instead of being called recent because it is found in contact with what is recent, is disengaged, and is made to tell its own story.

This insistence on going back to the source makes sense when put into the context of Indo-European linguistics, which saw many, but not all, of the world's languages as branches sharing a common trunk. Arnold, in his lectures, lampoons Charles Meyer's suggestion of a firm connection between Welsh literature, 'the *Nibelungen*, the *Mahabharata* and the *Iliad*'. Yet for all this newly-scientific sense of a humanity largely unified in its origins and inseparably mixed in its present condition there remains the suspicion of ancient survivals. Hugh Walker, writing in 1929 and harshly critical of Arnold's attempts to define essential racial characteristics, can still say that 'except in a few remote and isolated Welsh or Highland or Irish valleys, all blood in these islands is mixed blood'. His main point is the second clause, but the existence of the exceptions continues to haunt even such a sceptical text. It is this that haunts Machen's Wales, too.

The Indo-European tree is ancient and its existence is known to the meticulous researchers in the German universities. Yet it does not encompass all of humanity. The distant ancestors of those linguists 'Germanized' Britain and displaced, but did not exterminate, its original Celtic population. The possibility of a racially distinct human strain, still crouching somewhere in the Welsh mountains, remained; it was something in the dark beyond the floodlight of science, something older than civilisation. They do not even have to exist; the idea that they once have already unsettles the illusion of Indo-European dominance and hence of the inevitability of the civilised, modern world.

By the 1850s Arnold had already begun to withdraw from the modern world, seeing even the best of his contemporaries as pale imitations of the poets of the past and protesting that he no longer paid any attention to newspapers, the Victorian equivalent of boasting about not owning a television. The British and Irish attraction to their misty Celtic ancestry would continue. It had the exotic appeal of otherness compared with the more familiar, mainstream, Anglo-Saxon inheritance. W.B. Yeats introduced Irish mythology to Arnold Bax, the composer. Bax had been born in Streatham, South London, into a family with Dutch roots. He became absorbed in myth, teaching himself to read Gaelic and writing numerous pieces on Irish-Celtic themes. He said of one of his works that it

> seeks to give a musical impression of the brooding quiet of the Western Mountains at the end of twilight, and to express something of the sense of timelessness and hypnotic dream which veils Ireland at such an hour.

Once the notion had been raised of a Celtic 'race' that diverged from the same tree as the Anglo-Saxon in distant antiquity, its effect on the imagination of these edge-of-empire islands remained potent well into the twentieth century.

A particularly fanciful episode in this tale is furnished by the Victorian reinvention of the Druids, a development for which Robert Southey – Poet Laureate from 1813 until his death thirty years later – must bear some responsibility. His poems of fairies reached a wide audience in their day and he is usually credited with popularising the story of 'The Three Bears'. It was Southey that stoked the theory that the fairies were in fact descendants of the Druids, whom the Romans had driven into hiding, forced to subsist by theft and the abduction of children until they became the legends we now know. The emergence of an interest in Druids proposes more than a mere racial identity for the originals of these creatures: it also proposes a cultural one, since the Druids were believed to have their own religion, language and literature. At the time they were also credited with the building of Stonehenge, a replica of which was built as a 'Druids' Temple' folly by William Danby at Swinton Park in Yorkshire. Literary men like Southey and Sir Walter Scott may have popularised theories about

Druids, and their association with fairies, but they were building on the work of others. In the middle of the eighteenth century, William Stukeley, a Freemason who styled himself a Neo-Druid, was at work. Some of his *Stonehenge, A Temple Restor'd to the British Druids* (1740) is pure fantasy but it also contains very careful drawings and seems to represent the first observation that the monument aligns with the solstice sun. Stukeley traced the Druids back to a source ancient and eminent enough to impress his readers:

> And 'tis sufficiently evident, if we consider, that the first planters of Christianity in Ireland, immediately converted the whole island, without so much as the blood of one martyr. Nay, the Druids themselves, at that time the only national priests, embraced it readily, and some of them were very zealous preachers of it, and effectual converters of others. For instance, the great Columbanus himself was a Druid: the apostle of Ireland, Cornwall, &c. We need not be surpriz'd at this, when we assert, that there is very much reason to believe, these famous philosophic priests came hither, as a Phœnician colony, in the very earliest times, even as soon as Tyre was founded: during the life of the patriarch Abraham, or very soon after. Therefore they brought along with them the patriarchal religion, which was so extremely like Christianity, that in effect it differ'd from it only in this; they believed in a Messiah who was to come into the world, as we believe in him that is come. Further, they came from that very country where Abraham liv'd, his sons and grandsons; a family God almighty had separated from the gross of mankind, to stifle the seeds of idolatry; a mighty prince, and preacher of righteousness. And tho' the memoirs of our Druids are extremely short, yet we can very evidently discover from them, that the Druids were of Abraham's religion intirely, at least in the earliest times, and worshipp'd the supreme Being in the same manner as he did, and probably according to his example, or the example of his and their common ancestors.

In his earlier (and very fragmentary) *Itinerarium Curiosum* he claims no less than Pythagoras as an Arch-Druid and describes Druidic rituals taking place in the wood that stood where the City of Westminster took root. Stukeley died in Queen's Square in 1765; it is after him that nearby Stukeley Street is named.

By the time of Arnold's lectures the linguistic research being produced by the German universities was prodigious. It was one of the most influential scientific topics between discoveries about electricity at the beginning of the century and the theory of evolution at the end. Taxonomic classifications of languages had been undertaken before, as had attempts to trace the diversity of human languages in the present back to the miracle at the Tower of Babel, which many still presumed to be a historical event. Some held out hope that the regularities they detected between the modern languages pointed to features of the original tongue of Adam, spoken by everyone in the world before Babel. Similar enquiries tried to account for the dispersion of peoples and the consequent emergence of races in the world after Babel, especially the problem of how the remote Americas came to be populated. Such research, tied too closely to a literal reading of the Bible and lacking other evidence or an effective methodology, produced results that were as various as they were implausible. But it indicated the direction that the study of languages, cultures and races was to take in the next century. For the researchers were, above all, historical: they recognised, contrary to Aristotle, that things change, and that this applies even to very big, seemingly static things when the timespans are long enough. The disposition of languages in the present is not to be studied as some unchanging way things are but as something that has evolved and will continue to do so. The slow, organic process by which this was believed to happen meant that languages and groups thereof in the present bore discernible traces of their pasts, and this was the key to discovering how they got to be the way they are.

* * *

On 15 November 1841 an illustrious roll-call of luminaries lined up in Berlin for the inaugural lectures of the new chair of philosophy. They included the historian Burckhardt (who later became Nietzsche's mentor), the revolutionaries Bakunin, Marx and Engels, the scientist Alexander von Humboldt and a young Kierkegaard. The chair had sat empty for ten years since the death of Hegel, the most celebrated intellectual figure in Europe. They were all expecting to witness, for better or worse, a new, muscular phase of German thought. The new professor was expected to bring a new wave of optimism to the philosophical tradition of the idealists, which had begun to sag following Hegel's death and in the light of materialist criticism coming from the Marxist camp.

But when Schelling, the grand old man of German Romanticism, took the podium, it was a baffling disappointment. Schelling's lectures seem to have bewildered everyone in attendance. His emphasis was on the comparative study of cultures and religions. To some his ideas suggested empty intellectualism, no better than butterfly-collecting, while others saw in them a dangerous and decadent relativism where points of view have only relative, subjective value, and no absolute truth or validity.

Three years later, one of Schelling's students was translating parts of the Upanishads for him. Max Müller was an Indologist, investigating the roots of the languages and cultures of the Indian subcontinent. His father, Wilhelm Müller, had had his poetry set to music by Schubert, and Max grew up knowing various luminaries of the German cultural scene as family friends. He moved to Berlin where he studied under Franz Bopp and, in 1844, Schelling. Müller's work provides a good example of the way that the kind of comparative study that Schelling had exhorted, supported by the university system, had already begun to bear fruit, and would continue to do so, far outstripping the achievements of philosophy in the latter half of the century. In 1881, Müller published an English translation of Kant's *Critique of Pure Reason*, describing it in the introduction as the last arch of a bridge that 'spans the whole history of the Aryan world' and whose first arch is the Vedas. Müller does not seem to have been inclined towards racial theories, but the notion of an 'Aryan world' whose borders stretch from the Ganges to the Straits of Gibraltar was a commonplace of the time. At the end of the eighteenth century Indo-European linguistics was dominated by German-language thinkers, but orientalists were to be found elsewhere, especially in England, where the colonial project made the study of India both appealing and relatively accessible. It was appealing to government, as well: the notion of an Aryan world was transparently self-serving for the British Empire, where colonial rule could be justified as imposing on India the 'best' of its own civilisation, to which it was entitled. The study of Sanskrit absorbed countless men at the time in Britain and Germany and it was in this field that Müller built his eminent career.

The rise of Indo-European linguistics tended to legitimise a much older belief about the meanings of things: that they can be discovered by seeking their origins. Müller was invited to join the team that put together the initial proposal for an Oxford English Dictionary, which was commissioned in 1879, although it would be 54 years before the first edition was complete. The Philological Society, from which the effort largely sprang, had been formed in 1842 under the influence of German linguistic developments and the continuing interest in orientalism. Etymology became the key tool in the understanding of the meanings of words, a practice that continued to be used by the German philosophers of the early twentieth century. Supreme among them was Martin Heidegger, whose philosophy often took seriously the idea that the origins of words and their ancestral interconnections reveal a deep truth about Being, known in a time before civilisation but lost to an emergent modernity that spans millennia, a modernity of philosophical speculation and existential angst. There is a powerful nostalgia for innocence here, reminiscent of the pungent opening of György Lukács's *Theory of the Novel* (1920): 'Happy are those ages when the starry sky is the map of all possible paths'. The lost innocence is the simplicity out of which all of the baffling noise of modernity has slowly, organically arisen. Despite the marked differences in their thoughts and political fates, for both men human history aspires to return to such a unified simplicity, an integrated completeness in which philosophical problems vanish. Heidegger turned to National Socialism; Lukács, to Leninism. Neither ever fully repudiated their political allegiances despite living through the horrors they produced. (Machen, incidentally, came out in favour of Franco.) Perhaps the yearning for the simple and the repulsion from modern complexity were so strong that, as Heidegger later remarked, it seemed that 'only a god can save us now'. What their experiences teach us is that the quest for meaning in modernity is not best carried out by moving backwards through time to a point before the loss of innocence in Babel or before the Greek philosophers, or at least, that such a quest holds extreme hazards. The desire for a *deus ex machina* to descend onto the stage and resolve the contradictions of the tragedy being witnessed is understandable, but the Homeric world Heidegger and Lukács both longed for was irretrievable. They lived in the age of a distant deity, too stand-offish to intervene in human affairs: the God of Hume and Voltaire, for whom history is merely the clockwork unfolding of an inscrutable providence.

At 110 Guilford Street lived Horace Hayman Wilson, an imperial administrator in India who in his spare time contrived to produce the first Sanskrit-English dictionary and, at the height of the reign of King Cholera in London, to document traditional treatments for the disease in Calcutta. He wrote a miscellany of other books of a broadly ethnological character, especially on Hindu literature, and opposed the imposition of English.

German folktales began to be collected by intellectuals in the early nineteenth century. There was a craze for it. Shortly afterward, writers began inventing their own folktales, and these are often the works that are best-remembered today. If we reach back before the late seventeenth century, however, the story is very patchy. We find Latin or vernacular translations of Aesop's fables circulating widely from the sixteenth century, when interest in these texts increased for two distinct reasons. One was educational: the grammar schools required approachable Greek texts suitable for students in terms of both difficulty and content, and Aesop fitted the bill. The other was moral: the fables had always been loosely translated and retro-fitted with morals – often, Christian morals. In the heightened atmosphere of the Reformation, tools for the moral instruction of the young became more popular. Martin Luther produced a German translation of thirty tales in the 1530s; he found them so amenable that he suspected some of them of having been composed later, by Christians practicing in secret under pagan Rome. Melanchthon, the scholar who provided much of the intellectually-respectable theological undergirding for Luther's movement, encouraged him to complete the task but it seems he had bigger fish to fry. Aesop's fables, sometimes with their grafted-on moral glosses, remain popular among parents and educators today and later authors have taken many tropes from them.

Collections of Italian folktales had been published as early as 1550 (Straparola's *Pleasant Nights*) and, nearly a century later, Basile's *Pentameron*. Neither had large readerships. The tiny literate minority in Western Europe was overwhelmingly aristocratic, or aspired to be so, and what they saw as the crude chatter of semi-Christian peasants was hardly of interest to socialites of refined and Classical tastes. According to Jack Zipes, the first craze for printed collections of folktales was in France in the 1690s, although he identifies some scholarship that points to a gradual groundswell of interests in the salons sixty years before that. At these gatherings aristocratic women engaged in a wide variety of activities ranging from literary and philosophical work to songs and parlour games. Many of the latter seem to have had as their aim the general cultivation and improvement of the women – a 'polishing', as it were, akin to that received by men in formal education – and it is here that Zipes traces the origins of the emergence of folktales in intellectual high society. No pretence was made of recovering authentic tales: indeed, the ability to make them up *extempore* was often highly prized. Rituals of politeness built up around such tale-telling, and the tales invariably affirmed the values of the modern aristocracy. It is unsurprising, then, that when they were written down and printed, such works would be voraciously consumed by an anxious, emerging middle class.

These stories were collected and rewritten by Charles Perrault and published in 1698 as *Tales and Stories of the Past with Morals*. It is better-known in English by its subtitle, *Tales of Mother Goose*. Some of the stories are extant in other forms, while others – 'Red Riding Hood', for example – were adapted from an older oral tradition. Originally Perrault identified his young son as its author, perhaps because he was concerned that something so frivolous might detract from the gravitas of his public persona. By the time he turned to fiction he was retired (and out of political favour), but in 1671 he had fired some of the opening salvoes in the 'quarrel of the ancients and moderns', defending Lully's operas against the Classical strictures of Boileau and Racine and arguing that the France of Louis XIV had exceeded, in cultural value, even the heights of Greece and Rome. It was in the same year that he and the great astronomer Cassini, working under Louis' secretary Colbert, completed the construction of the Paris Observatory. So perhaps he was a little embarrassed by the indulgence of his fairy tales – as we would come to call them later – even though today they are far more famous than his serious contributions to French intellectual life. Philip Lewis has suggested that Perrault's success as a modern was his ability to 'domesticate' the more radical ideas in circulation and make them acceptable to a wider and more intellectually refined audience. His fairy tales, whose rather wonky and ambiguous morals contrast with those appended to Aesop in earlier centuries, are in tune with this.

Perrault had in fact been preceded by a wave of similar publications by the *salonistas* of his time; the 1690s saw the publication of numerous novels and novellas that represented 'literary fairy tales', stories with their roots in old tales for children but whose execution was sophisticated enough to appeal to adults. Dozens were published in the last decade of the seventeenth century; Perrault's is probably famous above all because of his powerful position in the French intelligentsia. They all seek to teach moral lessons of a decidedly contemporary kind; but they represent more than that. Louis XIV's rule had become despotic and, under the influence of the fanatically Catholic Madame de Maintenon, his country ruled by fear, catastrophically inefficient and subject to a regime of regressive and escalating taxation. These apparently harmless stories of far-off times offered an *aegis* under which the current state of affairs could safely be criticised.

Such tales continued to be written in the eighteenth century when, as in music, a poised, 'gallant', refined tone came to prominence: the voice of the Rococo. It is the voice of Watteau's paintings: languorous, self-centred, glittering, accomplished yet somehow also shallow. Soon sensibility would unseat this style, replacing its kernel of bitterness with a swooning rawness of emotion. Here the fairy tale gives way, for a while, to the Gothic, the story of explicit horror and fear; yet, even at the height of Romanticism, it will return.

The Grimms' *Childrens' and Household Tales,* their first collection, was published in 1812. Their stated mission was to preserve the trace of an oral tradition they claimed still survived the onward march of modernisation. It is tempting to blame this perception on a general drift of employment (and hence population) out of the countryside and into cities at this time. In England, this was the view of John Clare: an ancient, indigenous world on the brink of slipping away forever. Yet at the time the Grimms' book was published, about eight out of ten Prussians lived in rural regions. There is some evidence across Europe of peasantification following the industrial revolution, as intensified and specialised labour markets in large settlements, coupled with increased demand for unskilled labour to create food and raw materials, drove the unemployed onto the land to either farm or engage in rural industries. If the folktales they had collected had survived until then, it seems they were not in any danger of dying out in the coming decades: it was from Prussia and the German state of Hesse that the Grimms gathered most of their source material. C.W. Eliot's introduction to a 1909 English edition of the *Household Tales* assures us that it was

> the aim of the collectors, carried out with great fidelity and a remarkable instinct for the truly popular, to avoid all additions, logical or artistic; to retain as far as possible the actual language of the peasants, and to eliminate all foreign and sophisticated elements.

Indeed, until quite recently it was believed that these stories were transcribed more or less directly from the tales told by representatives of the 'folk' whom the brothers met on their travels. It is now known that they rewrote substantial parts of them, with an eye to Romantic aesthetics and German bourgeois morality rather than ethnographic documentation. Their versions of the tales went through numerous refinements between their first publication and the last one (in the brothers' lifetimes) in 1859. Hence, generations of studies of the ancient *Volksgeist* ('spirit of the people') which were conducted through the lens of the Grimms' tales have come to look more or less chimerical. But can we trust any supposedly transparent and unembroidered collection of folktales to be value-free? We would have to assume, in Linda Dégh's words,

> that the 'folk', as a primitive human contingent, unwittingly preserved elements of a forgotten, superior, national poetic heritage. Thus, for a long time individual contributors of folklore were only marginally recognised as reservoirs and retellers, not inspired artists.

On this view, it was the ethnographer's job to locate these pools of collective memory and, by linguistic and other forms of analysis, to purify their waters as far as possible, which amounted to stripping away recent accretions to reveal the tale in its most ancient form: 'to eliminate all foreign and sophisticated elements', to borrow C.W. Eliot's phrase. The drive to do this came from a uniquely nineteenth-century perception of the primordial world of our racial ancestors, whose nature is also our true nature, on the verge of disappearance under industrialisation, urbanisation and the other vicissitudes of modernity.

Hans Christian Andersen's first book of fairy tales was published in 1835. Unlike the Grimms, Andersen unabashedly presented 'new' fairy tales: stories that were original inventions, although many of the tales he published were in fact drawn from earlier versions. He lived in Copenhagen during the mid-century apotheosis of Danish cultural and economic power, as did the philosopher Søren Kierkegaard, who in 1838 published a famously scathing review of one of Andersen's novels (*Only a Fiddler*) under the title 'From The Papers of One Still Living', in which he paraded what he saw as Andersen's emotional and philosophical limitations as a novelist; he was snivelling and weak because he lacked any strong foundation of thought behind his values. He continued thereafter to hold a very dim view of Andersen's output. He was not serious enough for Kierkegaard, which may be why Andersen's stories have always been more popular than Kierkegaard's heavy, sometimes gloomy fiction. Literary jealousy? Both men were ambitious novelists. A small town like Copenhagen was not big enough for the both of them. Andersen's fairy tales, for which he is best-known today, were written largely as potboilers, riding the wave of popularity of works like the Grimms'. He considered his most important and accomplished work to be his novels for adults, which are now hardly read at all. He advanced his career by hobnobbing with the upper bourgeoisie and lower aristocracy in Denmark, and in his networking he made many friends but also enemies: the influential critic Heiberg's satirical poem 'The Soul After Death' placed Andersen in Hell, not being punished but torturing others by reading from his novels and plays.

Many of the Romantic poets of Northern Europe spent time collecting or inventing stories that seemed ancient. Goethe and Herder were especially influential in their interest in folktales and traditional songs. Achim von Arnim and Clemens Brentano collected many of the latter and published a set of folk songs and poems as *The Boy's Magic Horn: Old German Songs* in three volumes between 1805 and 1808. Undoubtedly, some of these are fabrications of the two poets, and some are heavily edited, although the extent of this remains controversial. In any case the collection was highly influential and its poems received musical settings from many prominent German composers of the time, including Mendelssohn, Schumann, Brahms and Weber. Later in life Brentano became a fervent Catholic, spending many years as secretary to The Blessed Anne Catherine Emmerich, with whom at least two miracles were associated (she was said to eat only the Holy Communion wafer, and to exhibit stigmata). Goethe's much-anthologised 'A Fairy Tale' and Wackenroder's 'Oriental Fairy Tale of a Naked Saint' were both translated into English by Robert Browning; so was Tieck's 'Blonde Eckbert', by Carlyle. These were popular works, and they were presented as explicit inventions in a folk-tale style rather than ethnographic documents. Fairy tales had an otherness and strangeness about them which permitted experimentation with darker themes: Rossetti's narrative poem 'Goblin Market' and *The Water of the Wonderous Isles,* a novel by William Morris (who lived on Red Lion Square), are both written like children's stories but deal with troubling psychosexual subject-matter.

> We must not look at goblin men,
> We must not buy their fruits:
> Who knows upon what soil they fed
> Their hungry thirsty roots?

As soon as literary writers encountered the folktale they transformed it and put it to use in reflecting the concerns of their own times. Indeed, interest in documenting 'authentic' oral literature seems to have rapidly become an academic specialism. The encounter with the supposedly ancient quickly became, for most, a gateway to the creation of the new.

Johann Gottfried Herder, a generation older than the Romantics, also collected folktales and songs. He called for a revival of the Gothic style of architecture against the prevailing Greek-revival classicism and investigated the origins of language in his attempt to capture the *Volksgeist*. He was looking for the primitive spirit of the people that lay beneath the external layer of civilisation (which was, by his time, associated with a literate, metropolitan internationalism). In this he drew on Rousseau's notion of the *beau savage*. Language was all-important since for Herder it went some way towards determining the categories of the world; it sprang from the particular historical, geographic, economic and perhaps genetic conditions obtaining in a society: 'Our whole life is thus a poetics, as it were: we don't see, but instead we create images for ourselves'. To understand who we are, or who someone else is, is a question of revealing and interpreting a buried sediment of myth and history. The importance of this for the future will be the internalisation it represents: myth is no longer something out there, to be discovered by philology and archæology, but something that might be found by looking deeply within ourselves. Some trace of *völkisch* origins are said to be found in every human being, even the alienated modern city-dweller. As late as 1931, for example, the composer and ethnomusicologist Béla Bartók could say that non-classical music fell into two kinds with very different values:

> We may connote urban folk music, that is, popular art music, as melodies of simple structure that are composed by dilettante authors from the upper class and propagated by that class. These melodies are either unknown to the peasant class or arrive there at a comparatively late time by way of the gentry. …The term peasant music, broadly speaking, connotes all the melodies which endure within the peasant class of any nation… which constitute a spontaneous expression of the musical feeling of that class.

By this stage, Bartók implies, urban mass culture cannot be ignored, but it is firmly contrasted with those rural traditions that constitute the authentic folk inheritance. Urban culture is alienated from its roots, which have been supplanted by a novelty-chasing, commercial changeling.

This goes some way to explaining the interests later ethnologists, anthropologists, and writers like Arthur Machen had in stories of brutal primordial rituals, including of course the practice of human sacrifice. As grisly stories they are not much: but if they are about something hidden deep in *us*, they become simultaneously more disturbing and more fascinating. The idea of an authentic cultural essence buried beneath the surface can be found in various forms in later German nationalism but also in English and Celtic nationalisms of the later part of the century: Housman's *A Shropshire Lad* draws from the same well, as does Machen's *Hill of Dreams*. These tendencies were already evident in the mythos of John Clare, the supposedly uneducated rustic whose elegies to an English countryside now enclosed and industrialised are among the finest works of English poetry. A fellow poet wrote in 1893 that Clare's poetry

> is what might have been expected from his long familiarity with rural scenery, and his intimate knowledge of country life. Simple as the song of a bird, it is best described by Milton's phrase, 'native wood-notes wild', for art it has none, and only such music as lingered in the memory of Clare from the few poets he had read... It is not the kind of poetry to criticize, for it is full of faults, but to read generously and tenderly, remembering the lowly life of Clare

In Clare the fantasy of the simple rustic endowed with miraculous genius provides a vehicle for mourning a golden age that has only just been lost, an England whose wholeness, suffused with golden sunsets and the rhythm of husbandry and harvest, still lives in the memories of the old folk. With Machen and Housman, however, the idyll is long gone, and all the more potent for being ancient. It is buried deep in the earth from which we rose: it may be in our bones but it's strange to us. For them, modernity has not merely separated us from our *Volksgeist*: it has radically alienated us from it. We cannot simply choose to embrace it, for now we find it frightening and dangerous. Yet it is not some specific thing, lurking in the forest: it is everywhere precisely because it is the spirit of the place. Even if the dark-skinned dwarven race of ancient Celts remain, dwelling in secret under the hills, it seems we broke with them long ago. The optimism Herder and the other early Romantics expressed for synthesis and reconciliation with this deep past has soured into permanent dislocation. The *Volksgeist* lies on the other side of a very broad and ugly ditch and the occasional glimpse, captured in a 'wild surmise', is the most that can be hoped for. It is what

I yield to fantasy; I cannot withstand the influence of the grotesque. Here, where all is falling into dimness and dissolution, and we walk in cedarn gloom, and the very air of heaven goes mouldering to the lungs, I cannot remain commonplace. I look at that deep glow on the panes, and the house lies all enchanted; that very room, I tell you, is within all blood and fire.

Arthur Machen, *The Three Impostors*

Freud would later call *Unheimlich*: the home we're not at home in, the haunted house in which a long-repressed trauma might be glimpsed. The return of the repressed is terrifying precisely because what returns, although it returns from within, does so as a stranger, as something we don't recognise and can't control. History turns against us. *Volksgeist* turns *poltergeist*.

※

Before he became a composer, Leoš Janáček had a career as a musical folklorist, collecting rural Moravian songs. He wrote his masterpiece, the Glagolitic Mass, in 1928, setting a liturgical text in Old Church Slavic. The work is usually identified as an expression of pan-Slavism, a movement for political unification based on a version of ethnic identity that was ancestral, historical and linguistic, bolstered by appeals to continuities of folk tradition and religion. The very notion of 'Slavism' built on the work of Indo-European linguists who had identified Slavonic as a major branch on the great tree of language, and in doing so legitimated the notion of a shared heritage; it was a small leap from there to a shared essence.

In religion Janáček seems to have been agnostic. He raised his children as Catholics and although he refused the extreme unction he would not be drawn into publicly renouncing the church either. Perhaps, for him, in contrast to the collective identity offered by pan-Slavism, religion was a fundamentally personal matter; this viewpoint was inherited from Romanticism and, before it, the 'enthusiastic' movements in eighteenth-century Christianity. The result, in the Glagolitic Mass, is an ecstatically Romantic hymn to the enchanted forests of central Europe: 'the church grew for me into the gigantic size of a mountain and the sky vaulted into the misty distance', said Janáček; 'the candles are the tall pines in the forest'. As Paul Wingfield puts it:

> The Old Church Slavonic mass text is evidently only the superficial framework for Janáček's distinctive mode of utterance. In this work Janáček expresses a relationship to God that I would describe as pantheistic. He avoids all things ecclesiastical; instead, a vivified nature-god sings his pæan of praise to the Most High.

Various reviewers of the first performances also used the word 'pantheistic'. The word does seem to capture the enchanted nature with which Janáček replaced the God of his youth. In it we find a curious contradiction (which extends well beyond Janáček) that cannot satisfactorily be resolved. The urban ideology of progress – steam-driven, industrial, liberal and surging forwards toward utopia – is in tension with the ideology of a rural connection to the soil, an ancient folk inheritance and traditions that are wiser than modern science. Yet we shall need to understand both tendencies in order to make sense of Romantic pantheism, a new-fangled form of religion born of the Enlightenment that looked back to a primordial past.

The Polish composer Karol Szymanowski died within a few years of Janáček, although he was a generation younger. Szymanowski was rendered unable to compose by the severe upheavals he experienced during the First World War, and so he wrote a curious literary work, *Efebos*, a universal story of the growth of the soul away from tradition, nationality and other forms of collective identity into a purely self-reflective state of solipsism, 'flowering as if by itself from the fertile soil of the human soul's deepest layers'. It is explicitly an erotics of self-discovery through the liberation and deployment of sexual energy, a programme deeply influenced by Freud. It echoes the many eighteenth-century narratives of human history as the maturation of a single person, from infantile attachment to superstition and religion through to the responsible adulthood of the Age of Reason. Yet in Szymanowski's story this process of self-realisation ends somewhere far removed from a straightforward Polish nationalism. 'Szymanowski set himself an immense goal', wrote Iwaszkiewicz: 'to reveal the mystical, Dionysian and Sufistic factors in the Slavonic. This is the highest goal a Polish composer could set himself'. This connection between an alleged Slavic *Volksgeist* and Greek and Middle Eastern mystical traditions is most dramatically demonstrated in his Songs of an Infatuated Muezzin. It suggests a wider view that has been called pan-European. Szymanowski was, perhaps, a relatively rare breed that would become far more common after the Second World War: a humanist mystic in the sense that he believed in the transcendental power of a common spirit in humanity which was not localised in a particular race or tradition. This is the intellectual end-point of the Indo-European process that began with a yearning for ethnic origins and ended with something much more unified. Yet the call of the modern humanist that we strive to 'be more fully human' in line with our birthright holds open the possibility that some are not fully human at all.

In Britain composers such as Ralph Vaughan Williams, Arnold Bax, Percy Grainger and (more obliquely) Frederick Delius indulged similar impulses towards what they took to be ancient and indigenous folk traditions and a luminously pastoral view of local landscapes. Very often these practices appear parochial but aim at a conception of humanity shot through with a vision of a common Indo-European inheritance. Remember the general tendency of all these beliefs: the older, the better. Hence retrieving some fragment of an ancestral memory that precedes current national alignments comes to seem more radical and more authentic. The further back you go, the more branches merge onto the main trunk. For Vaughan Williams it was particularly important that the English church find its indigenous roots, casting off imported airs and graces for a homely authenticity:

> The primitive music, which was made by the unlettered, untravelled, in our sense of the word incultured people, to satisfy their own needs; the people who Hubert Parry said 'who made what they liked, and liked what they made'; that is, after all, the foundation on which all our art is built up, and unless music is a natural expression of feeling, it is worthless. And if it is a natural expression it must surely come from people without any special training. I'm not speaking against special training – it is necessary – but without that natural desire, it's useless.

For almost three decades Vaughan Williams acted as musical editor of the English Hymnal, one of the standard Anglican hymn-books of the twentieth century. He explicitly rejected the idea that music for the uneducated had to be bad music because it had to be simple. 'As for simplicity,' he said, 'what could be simpler than "St Anne" or "The Old Hundredth", and what could be finer?' The composer's art, for him, consisted in refining an ore whose veins were only found in the deep traditions of the folk.

There is a rather different strand of Christian theology that seeks the truth in the origins of things, and which concerns the methods proper to the interpretation of the Bible. This was important in both the devotional life of the individual and the framing of church doctrine. Few doubted that the Bible, as the only 'direct' source of information about the Christian message, was of central importance for the faith as a whole, but groups disagreed strongly about who should interpret it and how they should do so.

Gotthold Ephraim Lessing was a Lutheran theologian who flourished in the middle of the eighteenth century; without doubt he was a product of the Enlightenment mind-set, although he never wrote out a systematic philosophy or theology. Indeed, he was notoriously slippery, employing irony (or a very dry sense of humour) as often as speaking directly. Nevertheless, we can say a few things about him for sure. He saw his tradition as set firmly against the church authority and 'priestcraft' so loathed by the Reformers and *philosophes* alike. For him, individual, rational inquiry was the spirit of Luther's reforms, and the spirit of true Christianity, so that 'no man may be prevented from advancing in the knowledge of the truth according to his own judgement'. Lessing is not advocating a myriad of different personal religions. He assumes that the truth of Christianity is a single unity, but that it is accessible only to the individual who devoutly uses their God-given reason to seek the truth. The image of the individual believer contemplating scripture alone, rather than being presented with it alongside an official interpretation in church, had been a powerful one for many radical reformers of the previous century, including the English Puritans. The addition of 'reason' into the recipe, however, would have sounded an odd note to them, a warning that something rather different was afoot. For many 'low' Protestants, reason and learning were not required for a correct reading of the Bible: the requisites were faith, perseverance and grace rather than anything so self-aggrandising as cleverness. For Lessing, the Bible's centrality came from the truths it contained, not from its being a sort of meeting-place between the individual believer and God. He despised 'bibliolatry' – anything that smacked of the use of scripture as a magic totem or fetish, a mere conduit through which the divine could act, like æolian harp-strings which the breeze of the Holy Spirit could agitate – and hurled this word at his contemporary, Johann Goeze, in the course of a furious exchange of pamphlets that escalated rather rapidly. By the second round Goeze was calling, in print, for his adversary to be arrested for heresy. Lessing, who was thoroughly enjoying himself, published further mischievous and inflammatory remarks calculated to fan the flames before he was informed that his local prince, the Duke of Brunswick, was going to have everything he published from now on examined for unorthodoxy. At this point he decided discretion was the better part of valour and turned his attentions elsewhere.

Anxiety about the status of Biblical interpretation, which lay close to the heart of Lessing's dispute with Goeze, was widespread. It would become more acute as the decades progressed. Although questions of interpretative method go back in Christianity to the earliest writers, the first doubts to concern us sprang from linguistic scholarship of ancient Greek and Hebrew. These came to be applied to the Bible with renewed vigour in the sixteenth century, when Erasmus and Luther produced and printed new translations of scripture. Both believed that they were providing more accurate translations than had been available in the Latin Vulgate version or, before that, the Greek version of the Old Testament texts known as the Septuagint. Catholic tradition held that these translations, like the original works themselves, were divinely-inspired. After all, any text's meanings are invariably transformed when converted into another language, even if the languages are close relatives and their respective cultural nuances are well-understood by the translator. The case of the Bible texts was clearly more problematic, and a reliable translation really required something like a miracle to guarantee it. Yet Erasmus and other scholars of the time had found what they believed to be severe inadequacies in the traditional translations and proposed to fix them.

If you sympathised with Erasmus's quest for accuracy you might have also been attracted to the movement known as Higher Criticism, of which Lessing was a founding figure. It emphasised the need for an understanding of the linguistic, archæological, cultural and historical context to inform biblical interpretation. It therefore became an activity that required a degree of expertise and knowledge; no longer was the lone, often barely-educated, reader to be trusted to come up with an understanding of the text that seemed right to them. At its most controversial it took into account what was known about the lives and opinions of the authors, which meant that rather than scripture being the timeless and undiluted word of God transmitted without intermediation, it came to look like the work of historical figures, divinely-inspired but rooted in a specific time and place. When the wind passes through an æolian harp, the listener can only discern facts about the wind given reliable information about the construction of the harp itself, which lends its character to the sound. So it was with the spirit of God, for which the wind was a well-worn metaphor, and the authors who, like poets, had come to be seen as conduits for the divine.

You might be surprised that all this ever took serious root outside the universities; then again, you might wonder why it had not been the way things were done all along. On the one hand it seems to cast serious doubt on orthodox ideas about scriptural interpretation and authority, matters that most Christians would consider foundational. On the other, it is hard to believe that the new knowledge being produced by the German university system could have been ignored by believers for very long. It may seem obvious to you that an understanding of the Old Testament requires knowledge, not of modern Hebrew, but of the language and ways of life of the time and place in which it was written. Yet the scientific (or, sometimes, pseudo-scientific) arguments in its favour were probably not what carried the day for the Higher Criticism, at least in Protestant Germany in whose universities it was born. Its popularity was probably due to its affinity with Romanticism and the continuing sense that the truth lay hidden in a past that was almost lost to us, only to be regained by careful study. Elsewhere the idea met with opposition: T.W. Davis has claimed that it was not until the 1890s that the Higher Criticism was acceptable in the English universities, which remained dominated by a rather conservative form of Anglicanism.

These quests for a unified truth in the distant past led in other directions, especially among those for whom any amount of learning or intellectual effort looked inadequate to the task of arriving at a reliable doctrine. In French Catholic Traditionalism, for example, we find a newly-potent revival of the idea that at the beginning of human history God had given divine knowledge to humanity, and that this had been retained, albeit severely fragmented and corrupted, in long-standing traditions. This, not reason, not archæology, and certainly not the discernment of the individual believer, was to be the sole reliable source of true belief. An emphasis on ancient ideas and texts inevitably followed, and from it came an acceptance of some degree of validity for several religions – especially, but not only, the Abrahamic ones – although not of course on an equal footing with Christianity. It was expected that structural or symbolic similarities would be found among human societies everywhere. This search for the collective truth buried in all cultures has a tendency to end in absurdity: 'a quest for Chinese legends of the virgin birth and Aztec symbols of the crucifix'. The quest starts with a sure step, from an emphasis on the teaching of the early church, but quickly, symbolism, mythopoetics, and syncretism (the merging of seemingly unrelated traditions) all threaten to run amok. This tendency led more or less directly to structuralism, which came to see the proper object of study in any field to be the deepest, simplest and most universal structures that could be found within it. The structuralist programme was all-conquering in the first half of the twentieth century across many disciplines, including anthropology, linguistics, sociology, musicology, literary studies, political theory and psychology. In the last decades of the nineteenth century Ferdinand de Saussure, founder of structuralism, was studying Indo-European linguistics and teaching Sanskrit, which continued to be his specialism throughout his life. His followers sought universal patterns in human societies, beliefs and customs, although as soon as each of them claimed to have seized hold of something solid it seemed to dissolve not long after.

All of this was a shift of emphasis away from the rationally-derived 'natural religion' of the *philosophes*, the book-learning of the Higher Criticism and indeed for Reason being a promising foundation for truth in general. For 'reasons' can always be questioned, and they seem to give rise to endless controversy rather than stability or truth. Tradition, on the other hand, offers the possibility that an originary truth might be recovered through careful interpretation. It is a project that promises to be based on empirically-observable evidence, and so potentially has all the advantages of science over philosophy. And all this was intimately braided with the political and social changes of the time, producing some strange compromises and accommodations. Consider Joseph de Maistre (1753-1821), a Freemason despite the church's condemnation of the society and a believer in extraterrestrial life. He was an ultramontanist; the *ultramontain* was 'the man behind the mountains', the Pope. Ultramontanists were strongly pro-papist and suspected of being anti-patriotic, since they supported the involvement of the church in state affairs: many observers considered the definition of papal infallibility at Vatican I in 1868 a worrying triumph for the movement. Maistre's political philosophy was that the only stable and peaceful commonwealth is the one ruled by an absolute monarch, answerable only to the Pope and supported by a rigidly hierarchical social order. The presence of the Pope at the head guaranteed a connection with time-tested tradition. Anything else, he thought, would lead to unrest, since any supposedly rational basis on which a government can be erected is capable of being challenged. He may have been influenced in this by finding himself very much on the wrong side of the Revolution; a similar experience was formative for Sade and other anti-Romantic critics of the *philosophes*.

Not all such traditionalists were ultramontanes. Louis Bautain (1796-1867) embraced a form of Catholicism associated with Pascal, reviving interest in the anti-rationalist 'leap of faith' as an essential component of true understanding, not only in spiritual matters but in all spheres of human striving, including aesthetics. For Bautain, Christianity was inherently mysterious, and required of the faithful a willingness to relinquish theology in favour of the traditions of the church which, by divine providence, contained more truth than all the books of the supposedly wise. For belittling theology he was condemned by Rome.

By 1750 the borders of the struggle between Catholicism and Protestantism had largely been drawn, and the key religious tension in much of Western Europe saw coolly intellectual Deists pitted against a quasi-mystical experientialism that was often perceived as dangerously unstable. The Deists reserved the sneering term 'enthusiasm' for those 'low' Protestants, Anabaptists, Quakers, Revivalists and other movements that relied on visceral experience rather than intellectual acrobatics. To the university theologians and the *philosophes* they were sects of holy rollers who had deliberately turned their backs on the great Enlightenment, without reflection. Enthusiasm stood for both vulgar emotional displays and certain modes of transgressive behaviour that, if generalised, could become socially radical. They were right: these groups and their descendants would be instrumental in many nineteenth century reform movements fighting against slavery, poverty and *laissez-faire* economics.

It is a short step from traditionalism to panentheism, the belief that God's purpose or mind is present in all phenomena. It is this belief that licenses the faith that is to be placed in tradition: the sense that providence or the Holy Spirit infuses all things, so those that endure longest are also truest. For a panentheist it is natural to see a uniquely human faculty – reason, or the imagination – as an emanation of the divine *logos*, and hence from there to believe that each individual human contains a divine spark. Something like this is in the background of all these strands of thought we have been collecting. Among the folklorists and some of the Indo-European linguists it is the genius of the race (or even the species), now smothered under layers of worldly civilization. Among the Romantics, the individual genius holds out the hope of being a conduit through which this powerful force can speak. The Romantics were unabashed about conflating God with Nature and describing the source of their inspiration as divine: they had taken the leap into from panentheism to pantheism, the belief that the cosmos is, literally, God.

John Campbell lived in the north west corner of Queen's Square. He translated into English Johann Heinrich Cohausen's *Hermippus Redivivus*, or to set out its full title from the 1748 edition, *The Sage's Triumph over Old Age and the Grave, Wherein a Method is Laid Down for Prolonging the Life and Vigour of Man, Including a Commentary on an Antient Inscription, in Which this Great Secret is revealed; Supported by Numerous Authorities*. This 'Antient Inscription' tells us that

> L. Clodius Hermippus lived one hundred and fifteen Years, and five Days, by the Breath of young Women, which is worthy the Consideration of Physicians and of Posterity.

The 'method' which is laid down, in common with much eighteenth-century science, relies on an invisible substance – the breath of virgins – that contains within it the spark of life:

> When the blooming Thysbe, whom the Graces adorn, and the Muses instruct, converses with the good old Hermippus, her Youth invigorates his Age, and the brisk Flame that warms her Heart, communicates its Heat to his: So often as the lovely Virgin breathes, the kindly Vapours fly off full of the lively Spirits that swim in her Purple Veins; these old Hermippus greedily drinks in; and as Spirits quickly attract Spirits, so they are presently mingled with the Blood of the old Man.

As a satire, it keeps a straight face throughout, even when describing how sophisticated air handling systems might be installed in boarding schools for young ladies, to pipe the kindly virgin-vapours through to small rooms in which old men would sit and gratefully inhale. Around such a simple idea, the book wraps all the complexity beloved of secret societies of hidden knowledge; and it finds its central evidence – an inscription that appears to refer to a 115-year-old man – on a Roman memorial, thus invoking the authenticity of age. 265 years after its publication, we found three websites (modern-day Rosicrucians, Zoroastrians, and Scottish New Agers) that quote from *Hermippus Redivivus* without noticing its irony.

In truth, the websites probably quote it *because* it is 265 years old, just as Cohausen himself infers credibility from the age of the 'Antient Inscription'. This invocation of the gravitas of antiquity is a popular device. Say you recognise that the modern world is inauthentic and shallow, its knowledge positivistic and its values utilitarian. You can try to solve this problem as Matthew Arnold did, by tracing ourselves back to a time when we were not like that. If that fails, or seems too difficult, exoticism offers an easier path and one, therefore, that was often taken. Here we find the truth about ourselves in a tradition radically removed from us; a stepping-outside-oneself by way of a sort of genealogical ecstasy. In Western Europe this path has generally led to Oriental exoticism and a fascination with Egypt. Never, of course, contemporary Egypt, but an imaginary Egypt of the distant past, almost infinitely mysterious and endlessly malleable to the demands of our fantasies.

It began while Plato was being rediscovered by the West in the late fifteenth century. Marsilio Ficino, in the Florentine court of Cosimo de'Medici, was instructed to drop his work translating Plato, and turn his attention immediately to another text that had come into Cosimo's possession: the *Corpus Hermeticum*, an eclectic collection of Greek-language documents allegedly from Alexandrian Egypt. They had been collected and bound together at some stage in the Byzantine Empire. Their author was said to be one Hermes Trismegistus, then believed to be a historical person who flourished around the time of Moses. His writings were therefore taken to be an ancient source of authority; perhaps of greater authority than the scriptures, since they were of greater antiquity and therefore closer to the wisdom originally given to Man by God. This was dangerous pagan stuff. It was probably Cosimo's considerable power that protected Ficino in exploring it. Yet he could claim an impeccable precedent: another work alleged to be by Trismegistus, the 'Asclepius' or 'Perfect Sermon', is quoted approvingly by Augustine in his *City of God*. Thus, it seemed, the sanction of no less than a church father was given to the exploration of subject-matter that might otherwise have appeared to be nothing less than sorcery. These texts were blended with some from the Neoplatonic tradition then also passing through the Florentine academy. This flowering of intellectual life gave the Renaissance of the sixteenth century its distinctive magical-astrological-alchemical flavour. While it is fashionable to scoff at this sort of thing today, it is worth asking whether the astronomy of Copernicus, Galileo or Kepler or the great progress in scientific and technical knowledge that followed would have been possible without it.

Ficino's magical practices were often aimed at turning the mind towards higher realities and away from commonplace earthly ones. They had a structure of initiation that was passed on to later theosophical traditions, with their secret societies and mysteries. Indeed, it would seem that the structure of the academy – a new invention in Renaissance Italy – owes something to the attraction of the Greek mystery-religions, closed to outsiders and providing hidden knowledge to those deemed worthy. It certainly seemed that this newly-rediscovered knowledge was opening the way to a new and glorious period of human history. The excitement which grew around the *Corpus Hermeticum* lasted for a little over a century in the mainstream of European thought before being rather suddenly relegated to the shadowy world of cranks and mystics. The death-blow was dealt by Isaac Casaubon, a learned Protestant humanist who fled the persecutions in France and found himself under the patronage of James I, England's most staunchly anti-magical monarch. In the king's employ Casaubon published a demolition of the myth of Hermes Trismegistus and of claims to the antiquity of the texts ascribed to him. Yet while the other aspects of Ficino's genre of philosophy faded away, interest in ancient Egypt only increased.

In the 1640s John Greaves published two important works on the pyramids and other ancient monuments, especially concerning the system of measurement he took them to employ. By the standards of its time, his *Pyramidographia* is a careful, rigorous survey of the ancient monuments at Giza, drawing on authoritative sources and direct observation. Alongside physical measurements, he attempted to date the pyramids accurately (but got this wrong). The older Cambridge scholar Joseph Mede (1586-1639), now remembered as a scholar of the Book of Revelation, had used similar methods to Greaves in synchronising known events with scriptural occurrences. The project came out of a desire to create universal conversion tables for systems of weights and measures, including ancient ones; but despite good scientific intentions, there was often an immediate political or religious agenda in the wings – usually about justifying some state of affairs, whether actual or desired, by demonstrating its great antiquity – and this coloured the studies.

The great polymath of the late seventeenth century, Athanasius Kircher, followed, dedicating much of his life to deciphering the hieroglyphics that had long mystified scholars. They defeated him, too; in his *Oedipus Aegiptiana* (1654) he offered up translations that are as bombastic as they are wildly wrong. Kircher assigns to them a whole heap of hermetic Platonism, of the kind Ficino would have approved but that was now very firmly discredited, and which has nothing at all to do with what we now believe the inscriptions to actually say. It would be 1822 before Champolion published the first reasonably reliable translation of hieroglyphs thanks to the discovery of the famous Rosetta Stone.

The fascination with Egypt, however, went on. It influenced absolutists like Louis XIV, who sought to emulate the pharaohs: Versailles, with its gardens sprinkled with obelisks and sphinxes, was the great Pyramid of the Bourbons. In Italy Bernini had incorporated obelisks and other Egyptiana into his sculptures, and where Bernini went the architects of the international Baroque followed: in England, Hawksmoor; in Austria, von Erlach; in France, Boulée and Ledoux. In a way that could never have been anticipated, the visual language of ancient Egypt became a recognisable motif of Enlightenment Europe. Perhaps it reached a zenith with the *Description d'Egypte*, a product of the Napoleonic campaigns with its mania for cataloguing and codifying; it would serve as a pattern-book for the eclectic architects and designers who followed. Ancient Egypt remained in the European consciousness well into the nineteenth century: the Romantic poets came to reinterpret it not as a utopia in the past but a ruin in the present. Shelley's 'Ozymandias' was a grim reminder of the transitory nature of things; not the *momento mori* of the Renaissance, with its reminder of individual mortality and the need for individual salvation, but a generalised mortalism, a sense that everything passes, including everything that now is. The lone and level sands that stretch far away induce a feeling of sublime wonder, that curious mixture of thrill and despondency that the Romantics saw as an opening onto the truth of things. The poem poses a quiet but definite challenge to all the narratives of progress – those vast and trunkless legs of stone – that marched so confidently through the nineteenth century.

Nothing dampened the fascination with Egypt. In 1859 Dickens wrote in *All The Year Round* that it was a national disgrace that while the French had erected *their* obelisk in the Place de la Concorde, *ours* was still in Alexandria: the obelisk of Tuthmosis III was lying in a ditch, having pieces broken off it by visitors to be brought home as curios. It had been gifted to the British by the Viceroy of Egypt as a mollification following their defeat of the French in the region, but had lain unclaimed for seventy years due to the considerable cost of moving it and its apparent lack of utility to anyone: such a long time, indeed, that the sands of Egypt had already begun to cover it up again.

The Egypt Exploration Society, still based at 3 Doughty Mews, was founded in 1882 'in order to explore, survey, and excavate at ancient sites in Egypt and Sudan'. At first, finances came from churchmen, fired up by the new historical impetus of Higher Criticism and eager to find archæological evidence for Biblical events. While some such evidence was found, the research led in another direction, away from the confirmation of existing beliefs towards a picture of history as a succession of civilizations that rise and decline with little sign of divine providence guiding the process. Sir Erasmus Wilson, who would become one of the Society's most important subscribers, personally funded the transportation of the obelisk of Tuthmosis III from Alexandria; evidently it had some utility for Wilson, enough to justify the heavy cost of shipping it to London and perhaps even the six or more lives it cost to do so. An 1870 edition of the *London Review* makes it clear, however, that this was no heroic undertaking by a single man: although Wilson may have financed the operation, it was a matter of national pride. As the anonymous author puts it:

> Tell our Fowlers or Batemans, our Cubitts or Hawkshaws, that all reasonable cash for the work should be forthcoming, and any one of them could devise an effective plan for bringing this grand Egyptian trophy to the metropolis… A penny ride in a Thames steamer would then give us a very pleasant pennyworth of Egypt.

It was finally erected in London in 1878, twenty years after Dickens had complained, and is better known as Cleopatra's Needle. In the time of Cleopatra it was already more than a thousand years old. For the Victorians this was about more than mystical yearning. It was national and imperial pride, an important element of Victorian Egyptophilia that is largely absent from the earlier tradition. As the British Empire did its best to claim legitimate ownership of the Orient for monetary gain, it justified itself by claiming what cultural or historical affinities it could; a miscellany of fragmentary connections that make the obelisk of Tuthmosis III and all the treasures of the Ashmolean, the Fitzwilliam, the Petrie Museum, the Museums of Edinburgh and Manchester and even the British Museum itself look like so much rubble in a tourist's pocket.

The Church of Humanity

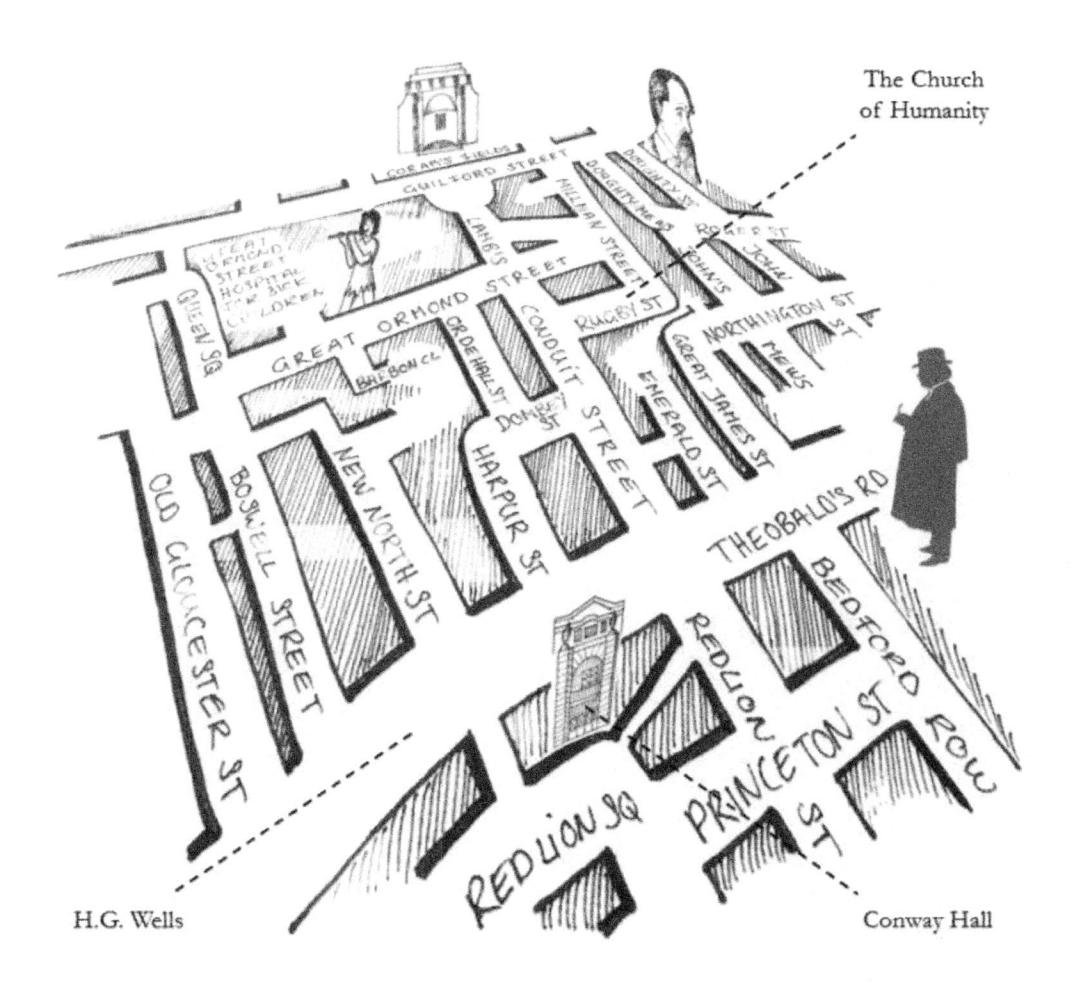

H.G. Wells

Conway Hall

INSIGHT

A great system of thought. The towering achievement of Enlightenment philosophy. This is how Immanuel Kant's philosophy is often presented today; but its immediate reception was as a cataclysmic destruction. *The Critique of Pure Reason,* first published in 1781, demonstrates that the disagreements between rationalists and empiricists that had dominated eighteenth-century thought represented fundamental, irreconcilable incompatibilities. The rationalists held that we cannot trust our senses; we can only trust our reason, and this is the only path to knowledge. For the empiricists, all that we have are our senses. They simply cannot both be right and yet, as Kant also shows, neither is satisfactory without the other. To the rationalists he said that 'concepts without intuitions are empty': that is, rational thought must have content, something to think about that can only come to us through the imperfect senses. The discipline known as metaphysics had promised a philosophical grounding for the sciences in pure reason but on Kant's account it was capable only of posing unanswerable questions and responding to them with 'castles in the air', and should be abandoned. To the empiricists, however, he retorted that 'intuitions without concepts are blind': it is impossible to go from the inchoate flow of data provided by sensation to knowledge of the world without some pre-existing conceptual framework that can make sense of all that riot of noise, colour, smell and texture.

In Arthur Machen's 'The Terror', Dr Lewis makes a similar point when relating how he had finally come to understand the manner in which the mysterious deaths described in the book had occurred:

> All this bears out what Coleridge said as to the necessity of having the idea before the facts could be of any service to one. Of course, he was right; mere facts, without the correlating idea, are nothing and lead to no conclusion.

In order to bridge the gap between the internal world of the mind and the external world of which we hope to have knowledge, this paradox had somehow to be overcome. Kant's own solution quickly came to be seen as a doctrine of 'transcendental idealism' that easily collapsed into a form of pure scepticism: the notion that each subject is radically separated from 'external reality' and can have no knowledge of it. We cannot even prove that 'external reality' exists. All we can know, Kant seemed to be saying, are the 'phenomena' that our own faculties manufacture for us on a stage inside our minds. In modern parlance, we are hard-wired to impose on sense-experience a certain kind of order before we can experience it as anything at all. External reality, on the other hand, is the domain of 'noumena' (literally, 'deities'), the mysterious 'things-in-themselves' of which we can know nothing even in principle, because if something is going to be an object of any kind of knowledge at all it must be, or be derived from, a phenomenon.

Such a reading puts Kant more firmly with the empiricists than the rationalists, and accepts David Hume's scepticism about the impossibility of absolute or ultimate knowledge. Hume believed that Newton's great achievement in positing a gravitational force about which he knew nothing was the realisation that he *could* know nothing; that it is as good as science gets to create explanatory models:

> While Newton seemed to draw off the veil from some of the mysteries of nature, he shewed at the same time the imperfections of the mechanical philosophy; and thereby restored her ultimate secrets to that obscurity, in which they ever did and ever will remain.

Responsible knowledge does not claim to go beyond the phenomena we experience. To do so is to indulge in metaphysics, the occupation of the scholarly fool. To make Kant agree so thoroughly with Hume isn't really fair on him, but something like this interpretation was widespread among his immediate followers; it seemed to say that two hundred years of philosophy since Descartes had failed to make a dent in the fundamental questions of how and what we can know or, indeed, to dispel the spectres of radical scepticism, relativism, even nihilism. It galvanised the next generation of German philosophers – first Fichte, then Schelling and Hegel – to seek answers. The response, which was both a product of Romanticism and its defining philosophy, came to be called 'absolute idealism', a rationalistic answer to empiricist doubt that made the history of the universe a story of the emergence of a total and complete *idea*, a perfect intellectual harmony that absorbed and resolved all apparent contradictions. 'The real is the rational,' Hegel wrote, 'and the rational is the real'. It took the individual subjectivity that seemed to be a 'dark room' in which we are locked and turned it inside-out, making it into the whole world. This new philosophy, developed in response to Kant, would dominate intellectual life until the end of the century.

The Critique of Pure Reason appeared in the context of other currents in thought that collectively threatened the sense that, for all its disagreements, eighteenth century thought had been progressing steadily in the right direction. Religious and philosophical controversies had forced many writers not inclined towards atheism to confront their philosophy's implications for faith. The Higher Criticism and ethnographic studies invited a dangerous relativism, since they foregrounded the existence of seemingly long-standing cultures that seemed very different from the European one in beliefs, values and all manner of practical matters. Who is to say that our scientific, liberal, Christian societies are better or more advanced than others? Newtonian science, and the development of biology and medicine along the same lines, had raised the spectre of determinism that had haunted Christianity since the time of Augustine but now seemed to stand more confidently on secular, even utilitarian ground. What room was there for human free will or the miraculous acts of God in a clockwork universe? There was also a dispute (in which Kant engaged) about whether theory, however rational it might be, could shed much light on practical matters: often those with great skill in the arts, crafts or technology seemed unmoved by fancy new theories about what they were doing. Perhaps knowledge, then, is altogether overpraised. Scepticism and nihilism became common bugbears and insults, and at least to some they must have looked like credible dangers. Western European thought was already on the tilt when the *Critique* came out; Kant's monolithic work pushed it over.

Immediately after Kant came Reinhold and then Fichte, both of whom attempted to repair the flaws in his positive philosophy, believing that it still offered a solution to the abyss that its negative side had opened up. They particularly wanted to solve the problem of free will in the context of the laws of nature that make the clockwork universe regular, predictable and hence knowable. It seemed to Kant's first readers that, despite his best efforts, either knowledge or morality may be possible but not both. Only if I have free will when I act can I be held responsible for my actions, but this seemed quite incompatible with the idea that the entire universe is governed by iron laws of cause and effect. The efforts of this first generation of Kantian fixer-uppers came in for criticism from a large number of German intellectuals – Feuerbach, Novalis, Hölderlin and Friedrich Schlegel – many, that is, of the early German Romantics now known as the *Frühromantiker*. In particular they resisted Fichte's attempt to find a foundational certainty – something like Descartes's 'I think, therefore I am' – on which he could rebuild a bridge between the phenomena of experience and external reality. The truth of any such foundation, they liked to point out, would have to be established outside the system, and since the system is supposed to explain how true knowledge is possible, it's not at all clear how that could be done. The result was that this first clutch of Romantic philosophers fell more in line with some modern readings of Kant. They saw his apparent 'first principles' as mere regulative ideals, important guiding lights that keep thought on the right path. Yet these were not stones on which a solid edifice could be built. The gap between the knower and that which is known appeared to be as broad and ugly a ditch as ever, and even the greatest philosophical mind of the modern world had not succeeded in closing it up.

Before Kant, German philosophy had been dominated by Leibniz. For Leibniz the key to understanding the deepest questions in the history of philosophy and religion was the intelligibility of things. He drew on a long tradition in which God was conceived of as rational – after all, He could hardly be irrational, since that would be an imperfection. Going deeper than this, God can be seen as something like pure rationality, the very principle of rationality itself, rather than just someone (like you or me) who has the ability to exercise reason thanks to the way our brains are wired up. Similarly, Christians had long described their God as actually *being* justice, love, mercy and so on. If God *is* rationality in these senses, His creation must be rational in every way – nothing about it can possibly be arbitrary or unintelligible. From this springs the famous 'principle of sufficient reason' that animated much of the thought of the time: for everything that happens there must be a reason, a meaning, a purpose. Things are not just the way they are: they are that way for a reason, and the rational mind can, at least in theory, grasp it. For Leibniz the apparent chaos and evil in the world appears that way to us because we are looking at it from a merely human standpoint; after death we may hope to see it from God's point of view and understand the underlying order of everything. The 'problem of evil' vanishes, just as a seemingly tangled mess of threads becomes intelligible when, looked at from the other side, we see the tapestry they create. It should be noted that this view of a perfect, rational creation tends to lead to deism, the belief that God exists but is not involved in the day-to-day running of the universe: having created the laws of nature, He sits back and watches as the universe runs itself according to His providential plan.

Thanks to Leibniz's curious reluctance to publish, most European intellectuals got to know his ideas second-hand (and considerably transformed) through thinkers such as Christian Wolff and Moses Mendelssohn. Though they certainly had their differences, the principle of sufficient reason reigns supreme for all of these writers. Nothing just happens, either in physics or in human behaviour: for everything there is something that explains why it is the way it is and thus makes it intelligible. Leibniz's important work in science, mathematics, philosophy and theology is unified by this one intuition, as is the work of his fellow travellers in the school of thought known as rationalism. For them reason can grasp truths that cannot be doubted, such as those of the mathematicians.

Immanuel Kant was by far the most important successor to Leibniz and Wolff. For some he was the most important since Descartes or even since Aristotle. His religious upbringing was in Pietism, a mainstream movement within the Lutheran churches of Northern Europe that traced its roots back to Johann Arndt in the sixteenth century. It shares many qualities with the Puritan sects in England: it is highly personal, anxiously pious and anti-clerical, placing a strong emphasis on personal experience and even something like sensibility. Superficially, such a background might have been expected to predispose Kant to the person-centred, experiential philosophy of Hume and his fellow empiricists. At the University of Königsberg, however, he was drilled in the dominant Wolffian philosophy. His critical project was to unify these two strands of thought into a single, more powerful synthesis. His scepticism about knowledge of those 'deities' called things-in-themselves, however, was a severe problem for many thinkers. Many came to believe that the Kantian project must end in atheism since the rational believer can only believe what can, at least in principle, be rationally known, and according to Kant such things as God's existence fall outside that category: he spends some time demolishing traditional proofs of the existence of God in the *Critique*.

And if this radical separation of God from our experience was a problem, so was the revival at around the same time of a Jewish philosopher of the mid-seventeenth century, a convert to Christianity whose ideas were so unorthodox that he was sometimes labelled an atheist: Baruch de Spinoza. On one reading, at least, Spinoza's philosophy identifies God and the universe. This is the position known as 'pantheism', the belief that everything literally is God. The physical cosmos is just one way of seeing things: one mode of the great substance, the one thing that truly exists. Another of its modes is what we call God. Like Descartes, Spinoza tried to develop a philosophical style that copied Euclid's mathematics in the hope of arriving at doctrines that carried the same quality of certainty as the theorems of geometry. Yet despite the familiarity of his methods Spinoza's conclusions seemed idiosyncratic in the extreme. He was widely-read but also widely-condemned and acquired very few defenders in his own time or, indeed, among the deists of the eighteenth century. Pantheism and atheism are uncomfortably close, and a Spinozist was what you called someone when you meant to imply they were an atheist and might harbour other dangerously un-Christian views as well. His books were not the kind you read out in the open and, since they are also uncompromisingly dry and serious, they were not much read in secret either.

A document appeared in the late seventeenth century which indicates the distrust with which Spinozists were held. It was subtitled 'In the Spirit of Spinoza', and it was claimed to be a translation of a thirteenth-century manuscript called the *Traite des Trois Imposteurs (The Treatise of the Three Impostors)*, a legendary text whose existence had been spoken of in hushed tones through the centuries, with authorship attributed to various heresiarchs. The three impostors were Moses, Jesus and Muhammad, and the text questioned the existence of God. It was one of the *clandestina*, or clandestine documents, handwritten in French and circulated anonymously. The English translation, which is now considered a hoax, was privately printed under the pseudonym 'Alcofribas Nasier, The Later', with '1230 AD' set under the title. Some have identified the Irish philosopher and satirist John Toland (1670-1722) as the likely culprit – the fourth impostor. The notoriety of this text lasted some time – long enough to influence Arthur Machen in his choice of title for his 1895 novel. Back in 1770, Voltaire had published his riposte in verse, the *Épître à l'Auteur du Livre des Trois Imposteurs (Letter to the author of* The Three Impostors*)*, from which sprang one of his most famous quotations: *'Si Dieu n'existait pas, il faudrait l'inventer'* ('If God did not exist, it would be necessary to invent him').

Goethe and Herder had been reading Spinoza together in the early 1780s. Goethe seems to have found the experience therapeutic rather than informative. He speaks of a kind of lucid calm coming over him as a result of engaging with these crisp, logical, unadorned texts. At this stage Goethe is wedded to a form of Classicism in which these formal qualities are valued far more than emotional or narrative content. As Matthew Arnold wrote many years later, in 'Spinoza and the Bible',

> Spinoza first impresses Goethe, and any man like Goethe, and then composes him; first he fills and satisfies his imagination by the width and grandeur of his view of nature, and then he fortifies and stills his mobile, straining, passionate, poetic temperament by the moral lesson he draws from his view of nature.

It is as if Spinoza was above all, for Goethe, coldly beautiful; it hardly entered into his head to ask whether he was correct. He declared Spinoza a tonic for his restless, poetical and sometimes egoistic nature. It also chimed well with his elevated view of the natural world as an organic whole, an all-encompassing Existence. On Spinoza's terms, he said, 'God is existence', and that means that God is Nature. This sentiment will later cascade through Romanticism. Goethe does not understand Spinoza as abolishing or naturalising the divine but – as through a translucent miracle of logic – coalescing God and Nature into two faces of the same single being. The social hold of Lutheranism was weakening in Germany; where an accusation of Spinozism had been damaging not long before it was becoming increasingly respectable. So it was that, at the end of the eighteenth century, Spinoza came to be read with sympathy among the *literati*.

Not everyone, however, took pleasure in this development. It was resisted in particular by those who cleaved to orthodox Lutheranism, who already felt besieged by the experiential pietism on the one side and rationalistic deism on the other; a new fashion for pantheism was the last thing they needed. One such was a member of Goethe's circle: a personal friend of his, one Friedrich Jacobi. Jacobi was already considered a leading conservative writer, so when in 1785 he published his polemic against the fad for Spinoza it found a large audience. It took the form of a personal attack on his fellow-Lutheran Gotthold Lessing, who had died several years prior but who had, allegedly, declared himself an adherent of Spinoza's ideas in a private conversation with Jacobi shortly before his death. Had he been joking or making an ironic point, as he was wont to do? Perhaps, but Jacobi took him to be in earnest and professed a fear for the salvation of his soul. Lessing was not part of Goethe's circle and, being dead, was hardly a potent threat to religious orthodoxy. The target of Jacobi's polemic was what he saw as an increasing Spinozism among the living.

Jacobi had just about the most curious relationship with philosophy as has ever been documented. He wrote that he considered Spinoza perhaps the greatest of philosophers. The trouble was, he believed Spinoza's philosophy was bad. Not that it was poorly-done, but that its consequence was so contrary to Christian doctrine that it had to be rejected. Where did this leave him? In fact, in an oddly satisfactory position. Hume had proposed, with convincing reasons, that knowledge is impossible. Kant, Jacobi thought, had proved it. Between our minds and the world outside lies an unbridgeable chasm. Knowledge is an illusion or, in his own pithy phrase, what seems to be knowledge is merely 'organised ignorance'. If we follow the rationalists with rigorous care and exquisite correctness we shall end in the absurdity – as he saw it – of Spinoza, the philosopher who pursued this line to its ultimate conclusion. Jacobi therefore believed that Spinoza's path should be rejected not only on moral or religious grounds but also because it provided nothing more than the best illusion of truth is was possible to lay hold of. His answer was a 'leap of faith' that circumvents rational argument, crossing the chasm between the knower and the world in a single gesture. While Jacobi's name is almost forgotten today except among scholars of the period, this idea is very much alive and remained extremely influential throughout the nineteenth century. Ironically, it is an idea he inherited from Lessing, the very man whose memory he was busy tarnishing in print.

Friedrich Heinrich Jacobi (1743-1819)

The next generation of German thinkers would be torn between Kant and Spinoza. They would find it hard to extricate themselves from the Kantian system, which was so crenelated with logical defences as to seem more or less irrefutable, but they would also be attracted, especially in their more poetic moments, to a Spinozan pantheism that emphasised a dynamic unity between God, the self and the natural world rather than a radical rift between them. A third strand, in a sense anti-philosophical and radical – perhaps even just exasperated by all this – would take the irrationalist option promised by the leap of faith. Something like the Spinozan approach would find, in Hegel, a champion as powerful and influential as any in the history of thought, and the organic view of nature, history and even religion would come to prevail in the course of the first half of the nineteenth century. It began to be forgotten that these philosophies about knowledge were all deeply-rooted in theology. In the 1830s a fourth road would open up: positivism. The unmissable figure on the road to positivism was, to put it mildly, a tumultuous character: Auguste Comte.

Comte was a man given to acrimonious public rows with colleagues and to domestic tyranny peppered with explosions of rage. Perhaps Anthony Giddens is right that his prose betrays little of this: it is severe, serious, meticulous and, some of the time, dull. Yet, especially in prefaces and other more informal corners of his texts, it can also flare up with an ugly temper. He is capable of self-aggrandisement at an almost Ayn Rand-like pitch, pouring scorn on other writers and presenting his doctrine as the inevitable next phase of history against which resistance is tantamount to delusion. He is not too humble to refer to 'my followers' in the preface to the *Catechism*, in relation to which he can only really be St Paul. In 1826 he delivered himself to Charenton, an insane asylum, where he fell under the care of Esquirol, the phrenologist, who by then had graduated from his training at Salpêtrière. Esquirol did not have much success with Comte, who discharged himself and by 1829 seems to have recovered under his own steam from what he later self-diagnosed as a disease of the brain. It was presumably comforting to him to think of the episode as a physical illness rather than a more disturbing, because less clear-cut, psychological one.

Comte's central work is the *Cours de la philosophie positive* (1830-42), a hierarchical taxonomy of all of the sciences that not only ranked them by their degree of advancement but also excluded some, such as psychology, on the grounds that they could never enter a 'positive phase', the phase that chemistry, say, had recently entered with the work of Lavoisier. To understand what he means by this phrase, we must grasp a few of Comte's nettles. Firstly, Comte particularly hated the statistical study of humanity *en masse*. This was a project he considered quite incapable of ever reaching a 'positive phase' because of its elevation of the group to an entity in itself, something other than the individuals that comprise it. In order to discourage people from taking up this study he gave it a deliberately ugly name: sociology. This stratagem was not successful. Secondly, Comte was influenced by Condorcet's *Sketch for a Historical Picture of the Progress of the Human Spirit* (1795), a work that saw the fulfilment of the human spirit not in some lost past but in the future. Like the *Sketch*, the *Cours* sees much of human history as a means to a greater end: the French Revolution, for example, as opening up the final period of human development. Prior to reaching this phase human endeavours had tended to pass through a 'theological phase', in which phenomena are explained in terms of the actions of supernatural beings, and a 'metaphysical phase' in which the priests are displaced by academic philosophers and the gods by abstract concepts.

Comte presents a progressive picture of humanity rising up out of ignorance and superstition. This is a sharp contrast to those strands of thought outlined in the previous chapter that sought a greater, more entire truth in the past rather than the future. It's a muscular optimism born of industry and empire, not the pessimism of an earlier figure like Edward Gibbon for whom 'decline and fall' was the principal theme of human history. Here philosophy looks to the future for fulfilment; the past once again looks primitive, 'Gothic', and its benighted inhabitants are to be pitied. Yet in the nineteenth century more remains to be done: in order to reach its 'positive phase', a science must turn away from the abstract notions of the philosophers, all those rationalists with their castles in the air, those Spinozists with their mysterious 'substance' and most of all the man Comte saw as his arch-enemy: Hegel. Hegel's absolute idealism seemed to disconnect *everything* from the empirical: he aimed at pure thought thinking itself, expressed by a piling-up of abstract nouns until, it must have seemed, the practicalities of life were left far behind. Instead, Comte insisted that a science in its 'positive phase' must focus on observable data and the system of induction that allows for the formation (and systematic improvement) of general theories based on them. 'Science deals only with surfaces, it has nothing to do with realities,' Dr Lewis explains in 'The Terror' – 'it is impertinent if it attempts to do with realities'.

This sounds so familiar that it is important to appreciate how it differed from previous philosophies of science. By training and by ambition Comte was an empiricist, and he therefore saw rigorous observation-based science as the only viable mode of human progress. Sentimentally, however, he had a lust for order and for grand systems: his philosophy of history is as fully abstract and totalising as Hegel's, for all their differences. This lust is, perhaps, a neurotic symptom, a dream or a nervous tic that the patient only half-acknowledges. Comte's odd, push-me-pull-you philosophy of science was hugely influential in part because it seemed to offer a way out of the impasses of the eighteenth century that Kant had brought to a head, and in part because it accompanied a surge in optimism about technological and scientific progress in Western Europe. This optimism was contagious and had already begun to spread to other forms of conjectured progress: moral, political, artistic and spiritual. Comte produced a *Catechism* of positivism: a summary exposition of the new universal religion in which a priest of humanity instructs an unnamed and suitably humble woman in the tenets of the new faith (Comte always maintained the intellectual inferiority of women, a biological fact easily, he thought, confirmed by observation). The *Catechism* revives late-mediæval notions of a universe ordered hierarchically according to eternal moral principles: an imaginary theme park for the paranoid mind.

Comte did not want to abolish religious practices in all their variety; he valued ritual, even fetish-worship, and what he took to be earlier, more primitive forms of observance, including those of ancient Roman civilization; at times he considered these to be more rational than the despised 'theological' thought of Christianity. Indeed, early on, Comte had been associated with a group known as the Saint-Simonists, who had cobbled together a socially radical programme out of the eccentric pronouncements of their namesake, whom a young Comte had served as secretary before his death in 1825. Saint-Simon's ideas had deep roots in mystical ideas, especially those about the complementarity of male and female principles, and it sounds an odd note to find them echoing through Comte's stiffly rational new religion. Yet Comte was not alone in seeing that forms of religious life retained a certain validity even if their metaphysical postulates about gods and eternities did not. Indeed, the idea of a 'secular religion', founded on principles that are rational, scientific or merely humanistic has been considered necessary for as long as people have rejected theism in the Christian world. This includes the deists of the Enlightenment and the atheists of today. The need for consolation, moral judgement, community and perhaps even a sort of psychological spirituality are not banished along with belief in a supreme being (or principle of sufficient reason). In 1870, for example, a Positivist School in the Comtean mould opened at Buckingham House, now 20 Rugby Street. It soon split from Comte's doctrine, however – nineteenth-century positivists being every bit as factional as modern Trotskyites – and became a 'Church of Humanity' presided over by its founder, Richard Congreve, as self-appointed high priest. David Hayes describes it:

> Ritualistic 'services' took place in a room to the rear, where people of all social classes met in praise of humanity, surrounded by busts of the great and the good of human history. The 'Religion of Humanity' had its own calendar of 13 months, with feast days honouring secular 'saints' from Socrates to Shelley, from Ptolemy to Priestley, from Romulus to Rossini.

The Church of Humanity lasted until 1932 and at its height coordinated several satellite churches in other English cities.

A few streets away, Conway Hall was built in 1929 as a new home for the South Place Ethical Society, which since the end of the eighteenth century had been associated with Protestant nonconformism and 'free thinking', a mixture of social radicalism, mystical visions and other manifestations, panentheism, emotionalism, extreme piety and a unified view of religion that accorded to some degree with the Higher Criticism. Yet by the time Conway Hall was opened the Society had fallen under the influence of men like Congreve to whom the specifically Christian elements of belief had come to seem primitive. Through the late nineteenth century the Society had become the focus of a strange, swirling aviary of exotic London specimens: liberals, socialists, anarchists, mystics, painters, trades unionists, abolitionists, theosophists, suffragettes, theologians, literary figures, aristocrats and Marxists. The inaugural speech at the new building was given by the writer Laurence Housman, who also founded the bookshop in King's Cross:

> While society advances toward rationalism, it should also advance toward religion, but to a religion different from past forms. This religion will derive from human experience, rather than from allegedly transcendental sources. Experience has actually led us, along the path of science, to perceive the

Conway Hall was named in honour of Moncure Daniel Conway (1832 - 1907), anti-slavery campaigner, champion of free thought and biographer of Thomas Paine.

limits of scientific understanding: to see that science cannot explain the origin of existence. Science leads, then, to a primordial sense of mystery, which can be called a religious sense. Also, the gospel story, whether historically true or not, advocates love, and love is permanently relevant to mankind. The sense of mystery and the cherishing of love are sufficient to constitute a new religion. Also, love is the more noble and heroic when the scientific perspective, which rules out ideas of immortality, is accepted. Finally, love should be all-inclusive, and therefore reject doctrines of nationalism.

In 1888, another writer for whom science led to a 'primordial sense of mystery' was living close to Conway Hall. H.G. Wells had rented an attic room on Theobald's Road for four shillings a week, with 'paper-thin walls'. He had come to London four years previously to study science, and was fortunate enough to do so under one of the great popular celebrities of biology, T.H. Huxley; much later, when Wells himself had achieved his fame, he wrote a biology textbook with Huxley's grandson. His fiction is an odd mixture. On the one hand, he said he used his writing to test hypotheses, by changing one variable and examining the likely outcome, like a carefully-controlled experiment in a laboratory. On the other, his fiction is full of mad scientists who wield a power so great as to threaten the natural order. These scientists, on the edge of genius and madness, possess a freakish intelligence, often enough signified by their phrenologically-swollen heads, which in turn symbolise the swollen power wielded by science in the latter half of the nineteenth century. Roger Luckhurst describes a changing sense of the place of science – at least in Britain – and its relationship to other important factual, spiritual, social and moral concerns. At the heart of this change he places the group of British scientists known as the X Club, of which T.H. Huxley, 'Darwin's bulldog', was the most prominent and outspoken. He does not consider the materialistic, often atheistic naturalism we often observe in our own present to spring from eighteenth-century Scotland or France, or indeed from the ill-tempered pen of Auguste Comte; he traces it firmly back to these campaigners of the late nineteenth century.

The 'scientific naturalism' associated with the X Club is not quite in line with the positivist project associated with Comte. Huxley, for example, advocated a theoretical substance he called 'protoplasm' of which all organic cells were said to be made, so that all living things were ultimately composed of the same stuff. This was the sort of metaphysical speculation up with which Comte would not have put. But the scientific naturalism of the late nineteenth century was a reaction against positivism, that 'Catholicism without Christianity' that had begun with visions of morally ordered society and had become, by their time, a tradition into which all new doctoral students were forcibly initiated. Herbert Spencer criticised Comte's attempt to systematise and order the sciences; Huxley said plainly that Comte 'knew nothing about physical science'. Spencer was particularly annoyed by the apprehension that Comtean positivism had been influential on British science, and several times stated outright that virtually nobody working in the scientific community in this country had any interest in him whatsoever. Perhaps he protested too much: Spencer had, after all, gone to the trouble of writing a monograph setting out Comte's alleged shortcomings. In a letter to Charles Kingsley, Huxley called the product of Comte's later work 'as big a fetish as ever nigger first made and then worshipped'. In the progressive view of human history Huxley had inherited (from, among others, Comte himself) this was tantamount to calling it backward, childish, regressive.

It was men of this temper who comprised the X Club, and it is they who lie behind many of Machen's grotesque and ridiculous men of science: 'And so we simply grin at [the paradox of] Achilles and the Tortoise, as we grin at Darwin, deride Huxley, and laugh at Herbert Spencer' ('The Terror'). Perhaps part of the reason for Machen's response is a sense that there is something of ecstasy in Darwin capable of delivering the same shock as Zeno's affronts to logic. Certainly there is no such thing in the domesticated, operationalised science of the others. Their denial of anything deep and inexplicable about modern science offends Machen precisely because *that* would constitute a genuine insight:

> Dr Lewis maintained that we should never begin to understand the real significance of life until we began to study just those aspects of it which we now dismiss and overlook as utterly inexplicable, and therefore, unimportant… If the mystery is inexplicable, one pretends that there isn't any mystery. That is the justification for what is called free thinking.

The X Club shared much in common with the positivists. The notion of human progress was crucial to both: not merely progress in solving the problems of this or that particular field but the progressive improvement of all humanity. Comte believed that positivism was automatically a political as well as a scientific theory, and naturalism was similarly concerned with bringing policy and social order under the technocratic reign of the scientists. This is what would happen to an extent in communist Russia and, later but more thoroughly, in Mao's China. Even today China is governed by engineers much as Britain and America are governed by lawyers.

The influence of the X Club has been so persuasive and pervasive that other ways of thinking about science now seem fuzzy and remote. In the eighteenth century, a standard way of doing science started with positing something like 'the ether' or 'phlogiston' and using it to make mathematical models. This was the kind of Enlightenment science that had proceeded from Newton's *Principia*, a curious work philosophically, since it posits a number of entirely metaphysical entities (uniform space and time, forces), wraps them up in new and exotic mathematics and uses the resulting apparatus to produce a stunningly powerful account of a wide range of physical phenomena.

Effective as it was, even in the late eighteenth century Goethe had developed a distrust for this way of operating. He disliked the idea of tracing natural, observable phenomena back to unobservable (and perhaps fictional) metaphysical entities whose existence was posited based on convenience rather than evidence. Goethe's cosmos was an organic unity, not something that should be divided into knowable and unknowable realms. He also disliked the system-building and totalising tendency of such a project, which seemed to be little short of theology. Most of all, though, he disliked the distancing effect that mathematical abstraction had on the ordinary observer. An observation begins, after all, with some specific experience: one involving patches of colour, shape, and movement. It is possible, and often useful, to quantify this experience in some way and account for the resulting quantities using a mathematical model. But this quickly becomes too technical for any but the specialist to appreciate, and that carries the danger of replacing the actual experience with the model and its data. The model becomes a fetish. Goethe did not disapprove of the use of mathematics in the sciences, but he did want to remind us that this comes second, and that the authentic scientific moment is the more immediate one that any of us can have. If one could reproduce in a member of the public that flash of insight, the mathematics can come later. But if you start with the mathematics, all but a tiny few will be immediately excluded. So Goethe's scientific method leans heavily on authentic, first-hand experience. Machen gives us a nice satire on the alternative, which ends up as mere deference to technocratic authority, when Dr Lewis remembers talking in the early nineties to a friend of his about the newly discovered X-Rays. The friend laughed incredulously, evidently didn't believe a word of it, till Lewis told him that there was an article on the subject in the current number of the Saturday Review; whereupon the unbeliever said, "Oh, is that so? Oh, really. I see," and was converted on the X-Ray faith on the spot.

This kind of seeing is infinitely removed from Goethe's – a kind of book-learning that rests solely on the presumed authority and expertise of others.

Recall that the model of science that German thought had inherited from Kant contained a sharp division between phenomena – things as they appear to us, constructed by our own mental faculties – and noumena, those inaccessible things-in-themselves. The noumena may be the 'real reality' but empirical science cannot catch hold of them directly, being constrained to the world of phenomena. The noumena are therefore posited as the things that cause us to perceive phenomena but are themselves inaccessible to science. Hence, on this view, we find the deepest truths about reality permanently closed off from scientific enquiry, since they are separated from observable experience by a heavy veil or, in Lessing's famous phrase, a broad, ugly ditch.

Goethe's *Urphänomen* is an attempt to resolve this apparently unsatisfactory situation by bringing the thing-in-itself into the phenomenal world. The term names the truth of a thing as it really is. To perceive it is to understand a piece of the underlying logic of reality. Of course, if this sort of thing exists it's hardly going to be perceived in quite the same way that a table or a raincloud is perceived. What Goethe had noticed was that scientists did not always tend to proceed in the methodical manner predicted by either Baconian or Enlightenment philosophy. Although stepwise progress is certainly a feature of scientists' work, there is something else too, today popularly called a *eureka* moment, that the philosophers seemed to have missed out. Goethe saw it as the result of *Anschauung*, usually translated as 'intuition'; in Kant, this is the faculty by which we perceive the world at all. Crossing Lessing's ditch requires a leap of faith that necessarily abandons careful logic in favour of some or other sort of active but indefinable receptivity. Intuition does not necessarily lead to useful or correct insight; it can just as easily produce muddle and mysticism. To be worthwhile it must connect with something genuinely and irreducibly true about the cosmos, and the bearer of this truth is the *Urphänomen*. This is the phenomenon perceived when you SEE IT – not when you see a physical thing but when you see a law of nature or a logic that lies behind more ordinary things. Looking at a blue sky is one thing, but, as Goethe puts it, 'the blue of the sky reveals to us the basic law of colour' if we see it aright. Goethe referred to many *Urphänomene*, yet over time he seems to have gravitated towards the idea of them really being a single universal one, at least at the highest level of what he sometimes called 'the Idea'. This would be no mere picture of an ordered cosmos standing still like a diagram: if the cosmos is a growing and changing organism, the *Urphänomen* is the logic underlying those processes, a changeless principle of change that is eternal or, at least, as old as creation itself. Science, as a quest for this object that is at once transcendental and immanent within the observable universe, becomes a quest for the truth that is hidden in plain sight, the truth that is right in front of our eyes but cannot be grasped. Yet in this way it can also become, once again, a quest for an ancient truth buried deep.

Goethe is widely credited with inventing the *Bildungsroman*, the coming-of-age novel, the novel in which a man or woman is analysed with respect to the forces in their past that made them. He was certainly not the first to take an interest in the chronological development of a character, but for him this theme had a philosophical importance. In the sciences, he thought, it will not do to look at something as it is now: it is also necessary to understand how it came to be that way. Otherwise, an understanding of it could only ever be partial and might be wildly misleading. A plant or animal, for example, must be understood from the perspective of its growth and maturation, and so must a human character. The *Bildung* in *Bildungsroman* ('formation-novel') has a double significance: it refers to the formation of the central character of the work, of course, but also to the formative effect the novel is expected to have on the reader, who observes this process of formation and applies it critically to him- or herself. This double meaning was emphasised by Karl Morgenstern in the 1819 lectures at the University of Dorpat that first introduced the term *Bildungsroman* into the critical lexicon. In German, *Bildung* had long been associated with Christian salvation, the process by which fallen nature is redeemed by divine grace. At the end of the eighteenth century the 'Weimar Classicists', among whom Goethe was a leading light, adapted this to their more pantheistic vision: grace was replaced with nature, salvation with organic growth and deification with realisation of the genius within the individual.

Johann Wolfgang von Goethe (1749-1832) holds centre stage amidst the glittering German *literati*. From left to right, Christoph Martin Wieland (1733-1813); Gotthold Ephraim Lessing (1729-81); Friedrich Gottlieb Klopstock (1724-1803); Johann Gottfried von Herder (1744-1803); and, in enchantingly fey pose, the youngest: Johann Christoph Friedrich von Schiller (1759-1805).

As a genre, the *Bildungsroman* tended to be conservative: despite Romantic notions of individual genius, the growth of the protagonist tended to follow a trajectory from childhood to adulthood, and as a key component, the integration of the adolescent into the social order. Summerfield and Downward have recently suggested links between the mainstream *Bildungsroman* tradition and Freemasonry; at the very least there appear to be strong parallels between the socialisation of the fictional hero and induction into a secret order:

> The mystery, the non-revelation, is an intrinsic component [of the *Bildungsroman*], as Goethe himself wrote in a personal letter to Schiller, 'it is a Machinerie that needs to act secretly not to compromise its power'. The Masonic *Bildungsideal* draws its strength from secrecy.

Although Arthur Machen was writing some time after the *Bildungsroman* genre had declined, this more general theme of transformative initiations into mysteries crops up repeatedly in his work. *A Fragment of Life* is the closest he comes to writing a *Bildungsroman*, in which a young couple gradually come to realise that their banal suburban life is but a veneer, behind which glows another world:

> And day by day as she went about her household work, passing from shop to shop in those dull streets that were a network, a fatal labyrinth of grey desolation on every side, there came to her sense half-seen images of some other world, as if she walked in a dream, and every moment must bring her to light and to awakening, when the grey should fade, and regions long desired should appear in glory. Again and again it seemed as if that which was hidden would be shown even to the sluggish testimony of sense; and as she went to and fro from street to street of that dim and weary suburb, and looked on those grey material walls, they seemed as if a light glowed behind them, and again and again the mystic fragrance of incense was blown to her nostrils from across the verge of that world which is not so much impenetrable as ineffable, and to her ears came the dream of a chant that spoke of hidden choirs about all her ways.

Machen's own ambivalent attraction to secret societies may have fed into this: he dallied with Freemasonry and some of its more exotic offshoots, including the Order of the Golden Dawn, although he left each group, finding their 'hidden knowledge' disappointing and their rituals rather absurd. They lacked, he said, that ancientness that might have guaranteed their authenticity, opting instead for modern inventions and clumsy syncretism. He found himself unable to get his fix of the primordial there.

Great quests for a truth hidden deep in things have their analogue at the level of the individual. There is even an ancient notion that learning is actually *remembering*. This goes back to Plato's dialogue, *Meno*. Here the character of Socrates performs a sort of magic trick with a slave-boy who, because of his social status, had received no formal education. He poses a problem to the boy: given a square drawn in the sand, draw another of double its area. (You may like to try it for yourself. You are only allowed some sand and a stick.) Socrates manages, simply by asking the boy questions, to have him arrive at the correct answer. Like a conjurer demonstrating he has nothing up his sleeves, he takes pains to assure his interlocutor, Meno, that he has at no point *told* the slave-boy anything, and the boy clearly did not know the answer at the beginning. The only explanation is that, somehow, the boy already *knew* the answer and was recalling it. How is such a thing possible? According to the theory Plato developed in other dialogues, each person's soul has always existed and always will exist. Before we are born it exists in a heavenly realm of pure ideas in which falsehood is impossible. Here, all truths reside, including those of mathematics, and the soul resides with them in eternity. When we are born, then, we already know every possible truth, but the process of incorporation in the body induces a kind of total amnesia. It is only gradually that the soul recalls what it has lost, and this is the process we call 'learning'.

It is a beautiful theory. Today, very few people would give it much credit. Despite the deep influence Plato had on them, all early Christian thinkers rejected it, for it required the human soul to have always existed: anything un-created falls into the category of 'creator', and that risks conflating the soul with God. Very early on in its reception into the Western European tradition, then, Plato's theory of un-forgetting was dropped. For a millennium and a half it was a dead letter, a token of the fact that even the greatest of thinkers have off days, yet something like it suddenly re-emerges in Goethean science: the idea that the soul has a built-in propensity for, or receptivity to, truth. The soul may not start out with a great catalogue of facts, but by its very nature, it *already* has built-in practical knowledge of how to lay hold of truth. Philosophers and psychologists may construct theories about how knowledge is acquired, but the reality is simpler: the soul is a kind of knowing-device, a thing that just 'sees' the truth shining out of things without reflection, without analysis, as a sort of reflex. We fail to grasp the truth when we let this slip away in favour of artificial methodologies. Children, uneducated rustics and, perhaps, members of savage tribes devoid of civilisation were held to possess easier access to the simple truth of things for this very reason. Those in the grip of religious mysticism or chemical ecstasy, too, were sometimes held to have access this simple, pure state, albeit temporarily. For the poet Gerard Manley Hopkins, the truth thus apprehended was a kind of electricity with which all things bristled:

> The world is charged with the grandeur of God.
> It will flame out, like shining from shook foil;

Hopkins wrote about the philosophy of his poetry, and used three technical terms that connect him directly to the Goethean Romantic tradition. The first is *haecceity*, a word with its roots firmly in mediæval theology. For him it refers to the individuality of a thing: its *thisness*, as he puts it. In the classificatory mind-set of the time one can look at a man and see a factory-worker, a father, a Protestant, an immigrant and so on, and thus subsume him under one or more categories. This is the work of sociology and statistics, the language spoken by the modern administrative state. Yet there is something inadequate about such a view, for by making him interchangeable with others of the same type it neglects what is specific to this particular man. This specificity is the *haecceity* that, for Hopkins, is the proper object of our knowledge. Abstract knowledge knows only about the abstractions it has invented; true knowledge sees things as they are in their uniqueness, and in a sense is pre-conceptual and pre-analytical. It recaptures a simple way of seeing things, now almost lost yet closer to truth than the operationalised knowledge of the utilitarians and the positivists. The *haecceity* of a thing Hopkins also called its *inscape* – a kind of internal landscape. He used the term especially of his poetic technique, by which he sought to capture the *inscape* of speech, its rhythms and kinetic movements, not by imitation but by a kind of primordial connection. To get at it, he abandoned metre, which had been the key structural component of English poetry for half a millennium, in favour of an older means. This was the 'sprung rhythm' of *Beowulf* and other Anglo-Saxon oral poetry, which predated the poetising tendency of English verse, with its imported Classical allusions and artificial elegance. What he wanted was not the refined, ornamented sensibility of the eighteenth century but the flash of true insight, welling up from the profound depths. Yet this description is perhaps misleading, for these truths do not simply come to us as passive observers. We must strike the right attitude. We must seek them in an act of will. He names this act of will: his third technical term, *instress*. So, although he uses these terms with considerable latitude, Hopkins has a system in mind. The *haecceity* is the uniqueness within the thing. *Inscape* is the way in which the thing appears to us:

> Each mortal thing does one thing and the same: ...
> Crying *What I do is me: for that I came.*

Together they create the possibility of insight but do not guarantee it. *Instress* is the way in which we comport ourselves towards the world. The moment of true insight is a kind of electrical jump or sympathetic resonance in which observer and world lock into just the right formation. It is without concept or beyond thought as all quasi-mystical experiences are supposed to be.

Less religious-sounding versions of the same general theory persist into the twentieth century. Ludwig Wittgenstein, for example, spoke of 'seeing-as' in a number of his posthumously-published texts. He observes that there is something immediate about some perceptions that seems to short-circuit all rational thought or, indeed, any conscious processes at all. We just SEE IT.

> I meet someone whom I have not seen in years; I see him clearly, but fail to recognise him. Suddenly I recognise him, I see his former face in the altered one.

Could we explain what we had seen? Often not. There is a promise here of a kind of knowing that vaults over the chasm between the subject 'trapped inside the head' and the 'world outside' that philosophy had worried at since the Renaissance, and that Kant had turned into the major theme of German philosophy. Do we sometimes simply find ourselves on the other side? Does this happen when we are least aware, least expecting it? Does it, like a dream, tend to slip out of our grasp the moment we try to catch conscious hold of it? And is it, as Hopkins's and Wittgenstein's examples both tend to suggest, to be found after all not in rituals or altered states of mind but in rather mundane experiences?

The two main branches of philosophy since the Second World War have been the inheritances of Wittgenstein and of another central-European thinker: Martin Heidegger. He, too, had a notion of a sort of immediate truth. It is altogether more fully-worked-out, being more or less the only theme of his staggeringly large output, yet it remains more mysterious than Wittgenstein's. Although Wittgenstein's occasional gestures towards mysticism are marginal, accusations of an obscure, experiential notion of truth stick much more firmly to Heidegger. The key word in Heidegger's philosophy is *aletheia,* the word the ancient Greeks used for both 'reality' and 'truth'. At its heart is Lethe, the name of the mythical river of forgetting that flows through Hades: *a-letheia* is un-forgetting and un-concealing. Heidegger often speaks of an unveiling of truth that takes place right in front of us, all the time, although we do not see it. When something exists it offers its truth to us freely like a gift, requiring only a special sort of acceptance; this is a structure he finds repeated in the works of many writers including Goethe (in the essay 'The Question Concerning Technology'). In his later writings Heidegger seems to become more and more wrapped up in an individual quest to become 'receptive' to reality in this way, to strip away all conceptual apparatus and simply become open to 'being'. This, of course, strikes almost everyone as a sort of relapse into irrationalism. It is the closed-off state of the philosopher-sage who no longer wishes to have doings with the world but seeks only a kind of transparent enlightenment. Heidegger's experience of having doings with the world was unhappy, so perhaps it is understandable, but this is where his earlier and more analytical philosophy almost inevitably led him.

The English poet Samuel Taylor Coleridge seems to have been well aware of the effect on the mind that imbibing too much strong German philosophy can have. In his *Biographia Literaria* he quotes an alleged anonymous letter from a friend:

> The effect on my feelings… I cannot better represent, than by supposing myself to have known only our light airy modern chapels of ease, and then for the first time to have been placed, and left alone, in one of our largest Gothic cathedrals in a gusty moonlight night of autumn. 'Now in glimmer, and now in gloom'; often in palpable darkness not without a chilly sensation of terror; then suddenly emerging into broad yet visionary lights with coloured shadows of fantastic shapes, yet all decked with holy insignia and mystic symbols

and so it goes on. A few pages later the same correspondent expresses trepidation about the prospect of following Coleridge any further:

> I will not promise to descend into the dark cave of Trophonius with you, there to rub my own eyes, in order to make the sparks and figured flashes, which I am required to see.

The initiatory rite of the mystery-religion dedicated to Trophonius climaxed in the cave that he refers to. Like many Greek mysteries, the secret was said to be revealed at this final stage, in the darkness underground; in the case of Trophonius, whatever it was, it was said to terrify many initiates into madness. The correspondent, however, is afraid that the mystery is nothing other than a self-deception. This is the opposite of Socrates's journey out of the cave into the light of day that represents the possibility of true knowledge. Terror, confusion, mystification, delusion: these are the dangers that await the reader should Coleridge expound his whole philosophy. All this is rather overblown, and at odds with the rest of the *Biographia* and with Coleridge's views on the excesses of the Gothic novel. The use of a third person narrator further suggests it is ironic. Kathleen Wheeler sees the construction of the whole *Biographia* in Gothic terms: a forest full of confusing sounds and densely twisted branches. Coleridge claims that it is precisely to spare the reader such exquisite agonies that he has truncated his account of his own system of idealist philosophy in the *Biographia*, saving it for its rightful place in a systematic work. For Coleridge the tree is a symbol of systematic knowledge: he has merely pruned it back to reveal a clearer path. He has no desire to immerse us in Gothic gloom even if, unwittingly, he sometimes does.

Coleridge never completed his 'systematic work' of philosophy. His scattered remarks on politics, religion and pure thought are plentiful and his attempts to produce a canonical statement of his 'system' are collected in his Complete Works under the title 'Opus Maximum': yet they are fragmentary. His readings of German philosophers are partial, sometimes perverse and often obfuscated, which is to say that he sometimes borrowed and adapted the texts of others without acknowledging his sources. He was rarely taken seriously as a thinker largely because his adoption of continental ideas was extremely unfashionable in Britain, where empiricism and its offspring, utilitarianism and positivism, reigned supreme. Despite some efflorescences of idealism in English-speaking philosophy departments, especially around 1900, German ideas have always been considered suspect there. In religion he shared a belief with the esotericists and the French traditionalists in the fundamental unity of all authentic human belief-systems. Yet he remained a firmly orthodox Anglican Christian (he was a vicar's son) and always pulled his philosophical speculations into line with approved doctrine. This gives his work an odd dynamic that seems to pull in at least four different directions: esoteric vitalism and ideas about 'life force', Kantian transcendental idealism, a certain relativism derived from the Higher Criticism and French traditionalism and, finally, high Anglican orthodoxy. The combination of all four makes it unsurprising that he was never able to pull it all together into a single system. Over time his orientation towards Christianity tended to increase, but these fourfold contradictory impulses remained. So it is possible that, for largely aesthetic reasons, Coleridge put aside the ambition to build a single systematic edifice and instead chose to create a mosaic of partial and not-entirely-compatible ideas. This was the Romantics' love of the fragment. He was interested in bringing diverse pieces of thought together, not homogenising them but letting them form contrasts and unexpected connections. This has much in common with the esoteric methods.

Many readers consider the most important philosophical part of the *Biographia* its theory of the imagination, extremely brief though it is. Coleridge makes a threefold distinction between 'primary imagination', 'secondary imagination' and mere 'fancy'. The primary imagination is the faculty by which the individual continuously and quite unconsciously constructs himself and his world, which Kant and his followers call *Anschauung*, intuition. The secondary imagination is the conscious part of this process that constantly re-creates and reflects on the process by which the primary imagination operates, and hence brings it to consciousness. Fancy is the dead equivalent of secondary imagination, not a process but a sort of arid storehouse of memories that the primary imagination has provided, and that may only be combined in varying ways. Secondary imagination, connected with the process of nature, may give rise to organic forms; fancy creates grotesque chimeras and portmanteaus, mermaids and unicorns. Anthony Harding suggests that these affiliations lead in a darker direction: a notion that secondary imagination has its historical roots in certain ancient, initiatory mystery religions.

It may also explain why he references Christian mystics so enthusiastically. At one point in the *Biographia*, for instance, he praises the theosophist Jacob Boehme. This is emphatically not for his visions. 'Many, indeed, and gross were his delusions', according to Coleridge, who provides a psychological explanation for them:

> Need we be surprised that, under an excitement at once so strong and so unusual, the man's body should sympathize with the struggles of his mind; or that he should at times be so far deluded, as to mistake the tumultuous sensations of his nerves, and the so-existing spectres of his fancy, as parts and symbols of the truths which were opening on him?

Boehme's value for Coleridge is his status as an outsider to the world of philosophy, who was therefore able to say what professional thinkers dared not, even if he could not say it with the finesse of the latter. He links him with the mediæval German mystic Johann Thauler, who studied under Meister Eckhart, and George Fox, founder of the Quaker movement. All three were Christian mystics who primarily spoke to a popular, rather than an intellectual, audience. One cannot help feeling Coleridge wishes to place himself in their company, in part because of his sense of his own inadequacy as a commentator on the forbidding philosophical systems of Kant and those who followed him.

Nevertheless, Coleridge saw Kant's *Critique* as a step towards the emancipation of experience from the tyranny of the empirical world. Strangely for us now (although by no means uniquely for his time) he saw Kant's philosophy as a vindication of the idea that life itself contained its own logic, and that it forces both the phenomenal world and consciousness to conform to it. This pointed to an underlying Nature that was more fundamental than empirical data – the phenomena – or even the noumena that were supposed to lie behind them. In his hands it sounds like a rather fuzzier version of what Goethe called the *Urphänomen*. He is aware that 'the system is capable of being converted into an irreligious Pantheism', which he links explicitly with Spinozism. Perhaps such an idea was acceptable among the radicals at the German universities but the Anglican Coleridge could not countenance it. Echoing Kant, he criticised Spinoza and the rationalists for seeking and claiming to find a foundational principle in philosophy where none had in fact been provided. All their proffered systems were subject either to circularity or to infinite regress:

We might as rationally chant the Brahim creed of the tortoise that supported the bear, that supported the elephant, that supported to the world, to the tune of 'This is the house that Jack built'.

He is, of course, quite right: 'first philosophy' always seems to rest on the metaphysics that Jack built. The age of Kant spelled the beginning of the end for the great philosophical systems: by Machen's time the optimism they represented had crumbled. Rationalistic attempts to deduce all of knowledge from first principles; empiricist insistence on nothing but observable facts; Romantic visions of the cosmos as a great organism; Hegel's sense that the universe was evolving towards a great intellectual unity; the progressive scientism of Comte and the positivists; all were, by then, showing signs of having cracked and crumbled. The promise of the Renaissance had been that knowledge, properly obtained, would enable humanity to pass through any veil of mystery. The great achievement of the Enlightenment had not been to realise this fantasy but to dispel it.

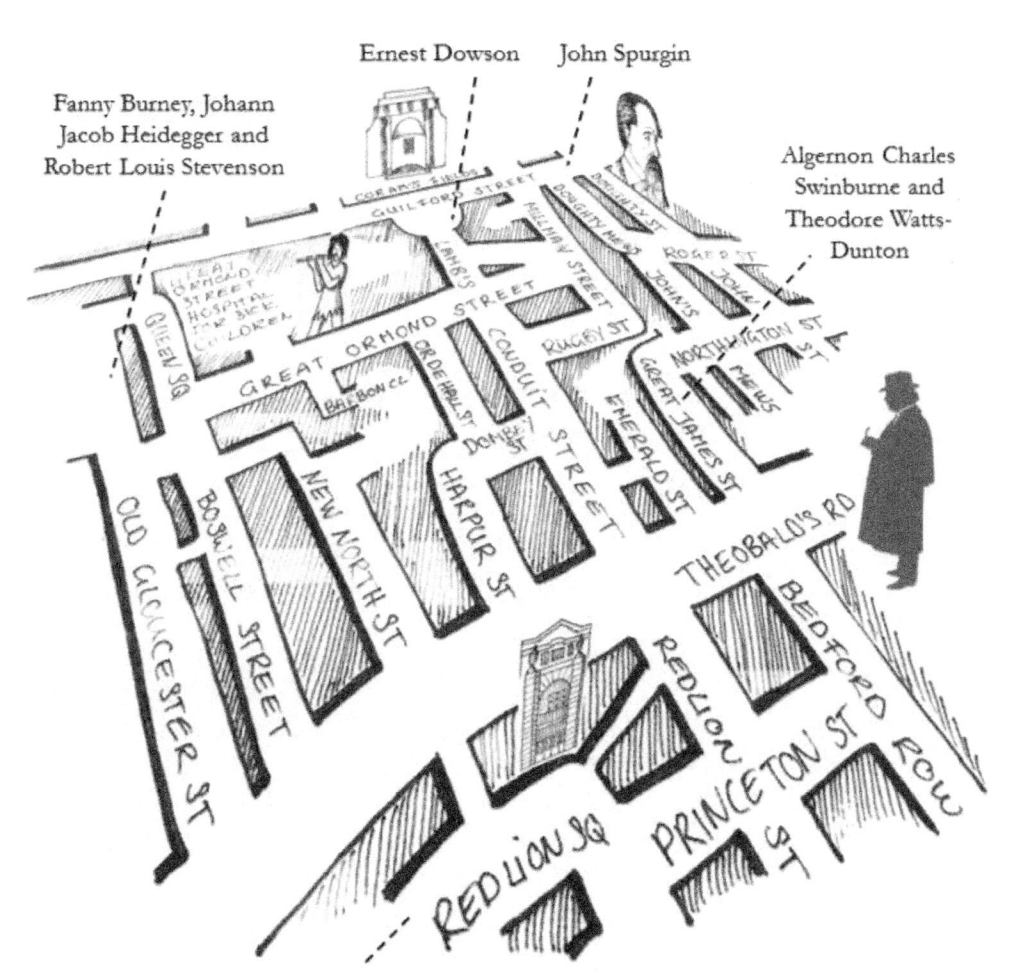

Fanny Burney, Johann Jacob Heidegger and Robert Louis Stevenson

Ernest Dowson

John Spurgin

Algernon Charles Swinburne and Theodore Watts-Dunton

Nicholas Unless-Jesus-Christ-Had-Died-For-Thee-Thou-Hadst-Been-Damned Barbon

ECSTASY IN SUBURBIA

Addison, writing in *The Tatler* on 21 May 1709, is concerned with the confusion caused by illiterate signwriters and suffered by 'men of letters when they first come to town':

> There is an offence I have a thousand times lamented, but fear I shall never see remedied; which is, that in a nation where learning is so frequent as in Great-Britain, there should be so many gross errors as there are in the very directions of things, wherein accuracy is necessary for the conduct of life.

This inaccuracy introduces practical problems for the likes of Humphrey Mopstaff, an unfortunate young man who 'going to see a relation in the Barbican, wandered a whole day by the mistake of one letter'. And this inaccuracy also blurs distinctions. Addison notes the ambiguity of the inscription – *rus in urbe* – placed by the Duke of Buckingham on the back of his house (now Buckingham Palace). This may either mean 'the country in the town' or 'the town in the country'. Which is it? The ambiguity, Addison admits,

> is not of great consequence; if you are safe at the place, it is no matter if you do not distinctly know where the place is. But to return to the orthography of public places; I propose, that every tradesman in the cities of London and Westminster shall give me six-pence a quarter for keeping their signs in repair, as to the grammatical part; and I will take into my house a Swiss count of my acquaintance, who can remember all their names without book

Addison fears the slipperiness of language is mirroring and even exacerbating a certain geographical slipperiness. This may be mere pedantry 'if you are safe in a place', but what if you are not? What if the place you find yourself in is suddenly a home you're not at home in? One way to tie down these ambiguities is through structure: the kind of rule-based grammar that was coming into vogue in Addison's time. Another way is memory, which is where that curious Swiss count comes in, who can remember all of the names of the signs 'without book'.

Memory had been the key ingredient in Locke's account of personal identity in his *Essay Concerning Human Understanding*, which at the time Addison was writing was new and very influential. The key moment is worth quoting in full:

> Suppose I wholly lose the memory of some parts of my life, beyond a possibility of retrieving them, so that perhaps I shall never be conscious of them again; yet am I not the same person that did those actions, had those thoughts that I once was conscious of, though I have now forgot them? To which I answer, that we must here take notice what the word I is applied to; which, in this case, is the MAN only. And the same man being presumed to be the same person, I is easily here supposed to stand also for the same person. But if it be possible for the same man to have distinct incommunicable consciousness at different times, it is past doubt the same man would at different times make different persons; which, we see, is the sense of mankind in the solemnest declaration of their opinions, human laws not punishing the mad man for the sober man's actions, nor the sober man for what the mad man did,—thereby making them two persons: which is somewhat explained by our way of speaking in English when we say such an one is 'not himself,' or is 'beside himself'; in which phrases it is insinuated, as if those who now, or at least first used them, thought that self was changed; the selfsame person was no longer in that man.

According to Locke the Ariadne's thread of memory is all that holds us together. For Addison, if the labyrinth of London is best navigated by means of written signs – *aides memoires* – then the anxiety is that the signs are deceptive. Certainly someone whose job is to maintain the signs in good order cannot rely on the signs themselves, but needs a more original source: living memory.

The 'Swiss count', Johann Jacob Heidegger, who lived at 20 Queen Square, was the son of a clergyman and certainly no aristocrat. He had come to London from Zurich 'in consequence of some intrigue' that led to a quarter-century of wandering in continental Europe. In the moralising words of a later *Tatler* editor, he 'acquired a taste for elegant and refined pleasures... united to a strong inclination for voluptuousness' that led him into the role of impresario. In London he in time became director of the Opera and promoter of masquerade balls, festivals for the Grand Lodge of Freemasons, and other high-society spectacles. Besides that he was noted principally for two things: his extraordinary ugliness and his prodigious memory. His ugliness earned him a mention in Pope's acidic *Dunciad*, in which he describes 'a monster of a fowl, / Something betwixt a Heidegger and owl', and it led to his death-mask being featured in Lavater's *Physiognomy*, a work that would later be influential on the phrenologists. Mr Heidegger, then, was no mere mnemonic performer. To someone like Addison he would have represented the vibrant heart of London society: a man who knew everyone who was anyone and who could navigate Westminster and its fashionable suburbs, in particular, like the back of his hand. He was at home in the place and his memory, even of something apparently trivial, offered the possibility of a fixed point in a world that seemed constantly sliding out of one's grasp.

Johann Jacob Heidegger (1666-1749)

In this book we have been tracing a faint line between madness and sanity, science and magic, religion and mysticism, experience and logic. The thin veil lies between them. In the eighteenth century, as opposites, we also have 'rural' and 'urban', but soon that thin veil expands to become not rural, not urban, but suburban. At first, it grows gradually, but then in a great rush – as the urbanisation of work reaches a peak and the railways make the suburbs viable for the masses who now travel daily into the towns and cities. Commuter land stretches, and for Arthur Machen (in *The Three Impostors*), before us is unfolded the greatest spectacle the world has ever seen – the mystery of the innumerable, unending streets, the strange adventures that must arise from so complicated a press of interests.

From the beginning, aristocratically-minded critics decried the uniformity of the houses and gardens of the suburbs and made sniffy inferences about the characters of their inhabitants: small-minded, cheap, aesthetically deadened, conformist, as alienated from the sophisticated pleasures of the city as they were from the authenticity of the soil. Clough Williams-Ellis called them 'mean and perky little houses that surely none but mean and perky little souls could inhabit with satisfaction'; John Ruskin described the residents of Sydenham and Penge as having

> no faculty beyond that of cheating in business; no pleasures but in smoking or eating; and no ideas, nor any capacity of forming any ideas, of anything that has yet been done of great, or seen of good in this world.

The assumption is clear: only the most mundane, most utilitarian of people and experiences were to be found in these new suburbs. They are places for people whose chief activity is a kind of work in which the Romantic sensibility could find no dignity: 'in those dull rows of dwellings', the maudlin Lucian opines in Machen's *The Hill of Dreams*, 'in the prim new villas red and white and staring, there must be a leaven working which transformed all to base vulgarity'. But many of Machen's other stories feature the suburbs in a very different light. In *The Three Impostors*, the antiquities-dealer Burton describes a suburban street late at night:

> Some mere protoplasmic streets, beginning in orderly fashion with serried two-storied houses and ending suddenly in waste, and pits, and rubbish heaps, and fields whence the magic had departed.

It is hard to know whether the houses have emerged from the protoplasm or are sinking into it. What is certain is that this is not the ancient and ineffable substance that the popular spiritualists of the time claimed to capture in their photographs. It is something more mundane that smells of brickworks and is presided over by streetlamps 'like stars', bathetic simulacra of cosmic magnificence. It is here, of all places, that Burton experiences 'some glamour of the infinite'. The city is civilised but its outskirts give way to something much more dangerous, because more ancient and less Christian: the countryside. As soon as one sees a wood, a mountain or even a stream in a Machen story one knows trouble is afoot. At climactic moments in the narrative nature has a tendency to become overpowering, overwhelming the character at the centre of events in a hallucinatory fog of indistinct terror and awe. The suburb is often the point of contact between these two worlds: on the surface, perhaps, a space of dismal mediocrity but potentially also one of transcendence in which intelligible modernity meets the strange and primordial.

We never actually see what lies beneath the surface of Machen's suburbs. We glimpse a glow as of stained glass here, or a sudden inhuman face at a window there, or 'a great ineffable beauty, concealed by the dim and dingy veils of grey interminable streets'. His literature is one that works by concealing and, in concealing, suggesting what it conceals. *Larvatus prodeo:* I advance masked. The phrase is a quotation from René Descartes, and refers to a path to truth that proceeds by deception, a way of seizing truth by the tail when it isn't looking. Pretending to be a simple soldier, then a man of practical affairs, Descartes creeps up on philosophy behind his mask. The critic Roland Barthes suggests of Descartes's mask that 'every passion, ultimately, has its spectator': the mask is paradoxically shown to us as such, as in an ironic performance. In the same book he gives a vivid description of the 'obscenity' of such acting-out:

> Evening at the Opera: a very bad tenor comes on stage; in order to express his love to the woman he loves, who is beside him, he stands facing the public. I am this tenor: like a huge animal, obscene and stupid, brightly lighted as in a show window, I declaim an elaborately encoded aria, without looking at the one I love, to whom I am supposed to be addressing myself.

It is in the suburbs, not the 'ancient fallen streets' about which still linger 'the grace and the stiffness of the Age of Wigs', that Machen's mysterious other world advances, wearing the mask of normality but also showing itself. Machen does his best to avoid the obscene display of Barthes' tenor, the kind of thing that from time to time happens in H.P. Lovecraft's stories, where the inchoate horror beyond the veil is made manifest as a banal monster, presented to us in its entire being, lit-up for our inspection, complete with tentacles, paws, 'red sucking mouths', rubbery scales, claws, bat-wings, membranes and (in *At the Mountains of*

Madness) even 'myriads of temporary eyes forming and unforming'. Although often described in a way deliberately difficult to picture, Lovecraft's vision is too explicit for Machen. It is also too uncompromisingly evil, a Freudian Id that breaks through into consciousness wanting nothing but to devour and destroy. What Machen's suburbs reveal behind their veil, what they disclose by wearing the mask of normality, is something more ambiguous: frightening, unfamiliar but perhaps also beautiful.

Yet on the surface the suburbs typify normality. Towards the west end of Guilford Street, beyond that place where King George III was once locked away with his demons, lies Queen Square, 'a little enclosure of tall trees and comely brick houses' as Robert Louis Stevenson once described it, which

> seems to be have been set apart for the humanities of life and alleviation of all hard destinies. As you go round it, you read, upon every second door plate, some offer of help to the afflicted. There are hospitals for sick children, where you may see a little white-faced convalescent on the balcony talking to his brothers and sisters and the baby, who are below there on a visit to him… There is something grave and kindly about the aspect of the Square that does not belie the grave and kindly character of what goes on there day by day.

On Queen Square lived the novelist Fanny Burney, who also worked as Assistant Keeper of the Wardrobe to Queen Charlotte and observed King George's madness first-hand. In 1832 she produced a memoir of her father based on his own notes and her recollections. In it she describes the family's relocation from Queen Square to a house in St Martin's Street that had once belonged to Isaac Newton, and which came complete with an observatory on the roof, commanding panoramic views of London. Dr Burney, according to his daughter, restored this amenity to something like its former state not once but, after severe damage, twice: he 'would have thought himself a ruthless Goth, had he permitted the *sanctum sanctorum* of the developer of the skies in their embodied movements, to have been scattered to nonentity through his neglect or parsimony'. Yet to acquire their enviable urban

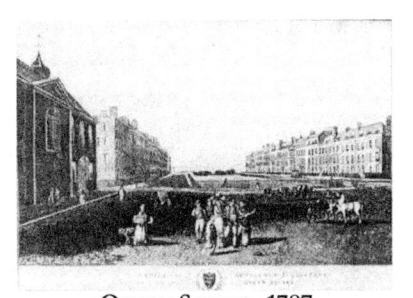

Queen Square, 1787

Queen Square, Bloomsbury. The inaugural meeting for The Society for the Protection of Ancient Buildings, founded by William Morris in 1877, was held here; from 1936-81 it resided at 55-57 Great Ormond Street.

view over London, the Burneys had to sacrifice another, very different vista. Until the late eighteenth century, the north side of Queen Square had been left undeveloped, affording a view of 'the hills, ever verdant and smiling, of Hampstead and Highgate; which, at that period, in unobstructed view, had faced his dwelling in Queen-square'. Residents enjoyed views north over open fields until the Foundling Hospital ran short of funds and turned to residential development of its land; and with that, this bucolic vista vanished, closed in by the growth of the city. It now seems impossibly hemmed-in by miles of suburban sprawl.

When fields are turned over to housing they change beyond recognition. Yet the meanings of the adjoining areas are also altered. A century before, the development of Red Lion Square in 1684 by Nicholas Barbon provoked residents of Gray's Inn to throw bricks at the builders, not because their land was being built on or altered in any way but because its meaning and value were being affected by what was going on next door. Their own vistas were being swallowed up by Queen Square and its environs, and over the course of the next two hundred years one liminal district after another would lose its sylvan view, with the fantasy of idyllic country living that went with it, to more brick houses, more factories, more railway stations, as London – and every other major city in Britain – expanded to absorb the influx of labour demanded by industrial capital. Between 1871 and 1911 the population of Greater London almost doubled, to more than seven million. Once the vistas of the countryside had been walled-up they must have come to seem strange, backward, primitive even; comical, certainly, and sometimes also frightening. Novelists like Lawrence and Hardy became popular among urban readers by depicting a country life that was hard, pinched and lacking in ornament in a way that would be mercilessly parodied by Stella Gibbons's *Cold Comfort Farm* (1932). Urban life could be as harsh as it had been in the fields, but by contrast the suburban world offered a kind of domesticated tranquillity.

In this book we have been suggesting – with the illustrious lawyer Thomas Erskine on our side – that the opposite of madness is rationality, and the limitations of rationalism has been one of our topics. Yet there is another, more recent candidate for this role: normality. Fiery Victorian and Edwardian tirades against the suburbs identified them as deserts of the creative genius but did not chiefly condemn them as *rational*: they instead called them dreary, dismal, ordinary, run-of-the-mill, *normal*. The sensitive reader of Ruskin would hardly wish to be found among the shuffling masses whose minutely uninspired lives T.S. Eliot later unkindly satirised in *The Waste Land*. For the Romantic, normality is the opposite of madness, madness the possibility of genius. This continues to run as a thread through twentieth-century culture: the suspicion that we all have a divine spark within that we do our best to extinguish, and that most have succeeded in putting out at the expense of their happiness and fulfilment as human beings. All this, Ian Hacking has argued, was an invention of the Romantic age.

The origins of the word 'normal' are somewhat veiled but the most usual derivation is from the Latin *normalis* (conforming to a rule or standard) and thence from the Greek *gnomon* (a carpenter's L-square). In English the word is one of thousands of 'inkhorn terms' coined by writers without precedent in spoken language during the explosion of English vocabulary in the sixteenth century. So it has always carried two meanings: the second, modern sense, meaning something that is in some way accepted, expected, conventional or standard, did not become widespread until the early nineteenth century. Just before that, however, it acquired a new mathematical meaning that was to become hugely influential. In mathematics, 'normal' had long been a very common word that could have various technical meanings but always carried the original sense of something being at right angles to something else. The new meaning it acquired came with a discovery by Carl Friedrich Gauss, born in the decade of the Romantic generation and one of the greatest mathematicians who ever lived. Gauss studied the tendency for errors or deviations from the average to behave in predictable ways. The result was what became known as 'the normal distribution' which, in the simplest possible case, looks like the familiar bell curve: a curve that is highest in the middle and elegantly falls away on either side.

Say I toss a fair coin ten times and record how many heads I get. This is one trial. Now I repeat this trial many times and record how many times I get each outcome. I'll expect to get five heads most often; then I'll get four slightly less often and six about the same number of times, three and seven less often again, two and eight quite rarely, one and nine very rarely, ten and zero almost never (but not absolutely never). The resulting plot will come up in a symmetrical hump with its highest point at five, the mean outcome. From this plot we can easily calculate answers to questions like the following: which is more likely, that we will get exactly five heads or more than six? It is called the 'binomial distribution' and

**Carl Friedrich Gauss (1777-1855) and his bell curve.
Detail from a 10 Deutsche Mark note, 1999**

is mathematically rather convenient to work with, and was known about long before Gauss.

Now imagine a trial consists of fifty tosses instead of ten. The mean will be 25 and the outcomes will, again, be spread equally either side of 25 with the same bell-shaped pattern, but this time the shape will be smoother because there are more possibilities. Now imagine there are a thousand tosses in a trial, or a million, and so on. The resulting series of curves converges towards the one that describes what happens if there are an infinite number of coin tosses. This curve is the normal distribution. It's useful for dealing with continuous variables like height and weight that can vary by arbitrarily small fractional values, rather than things we can count like the number of heads in a coin-tossing trial. This curve is what Gauss discovered; it was a discovery that was only possible thanks to the development of calculus in the eighteenth century, beginning with the innovations of Newton and Leibniz.

Today the normal distribution is a vital component of the field that came to be known as 'statistics'. The word is derived from Latin and Italian words meaning statecraft. In the eighteenth century the newly-coined German word *Statistik* meant the study of the condition of the state and, in particular, the resources available to it should it need to go to war. Access to chemicals and materials, numbers of healthy men of fighting age, costs and revenues and so on were counted up, and this process owed far more to Europe's increasingly large and capable bureaucracies than to mathematical innovation. It was difficult: many of these things, especially those relating to population and demography, were fuzzy and could not literally be counted: in the simplest imaginable case, how do we decide who inhabits France and who doesn't? Many of these variables were, in fact, defined by the very departments tasked with counting them. In the newly-expanded Prussia and, superlatively, in the Napoleonic empire, the departments of statistics became important arms of government.

The gathering of numerical data was sometimes done in terms of discovering 'constants' of nature like Newton's famous G (the universal gravitational constant). These included things like numerical facts about the periods of the planets' orbits, properties of materials such as density and melting point, number of species of animals, rate of work produced by labourers and so on. The notion that these things might have histories, and therefore not be constants at all, emerged slowly and sporadically. Today we believe that constants of nature are rather rare and we still do not know how many, if any, are truly constant over extremely long time periods and across large cosmic distances.

Something else important began to happen as the tables of the 'condition of the state' were drawn up and, to a limited extent, made available for comparison. The idea emerged that a people – a 'race' in the most general sense – could be defined not by qualitative properties like temperament, culture or history but by *averages* of measurements, giving rise to abstract objects like the 'average Frenchman', the 'average Englishman' and so on. The philosophical issue here is that we pass quite subtly from real quantities – the measured heights, say, of some specific people – to a completely manufactured one – their average height, approximated through many trials of measurement – that comes to be seen as something actual.

The original problem that gave rise to the normal distribution was one of measurement in physics. It began with the old idea from astronomy that many individual observations, each plagued by an unknown error, could in aggregate yield a number closer to the truth than any actual observation taken on its own. Imperfections in equipment meant that such errors were inescapable, but taking what we would later call a 'statistical' approach meant that, all things being equal, the errors ought to average out and leave us with something close to the best measurement. Human beings, however, do not seem to vary from the mean because of some kind of error but because of many, many tiny mechanical causes, different in the case of each person, that make us the way we are. In each case the presence of a cause is effectively random, like getting tails in a coin-toss. In the absence of any of them we would obtain *l'homme type*, the average man. This made the empiricists uncomfortable: it sounded as if the object of study was moving away from the concrete towards some abstract object that had been conjured up by means of equations. Perhaps even worse, this view could lead to fatalism. If mechanistic causes explained the suicide rate (as they were taken to do) will not the same number of people end their lives next year, as destined by the iron laws of physics? Is the mean a kind of law of nature to which we are forced to conform, more or less closely, something that exerts an irresistible gravitational attraction? Perhaps in some cases the average came to look like an ideal, capable only of very gradual improvement, because of a sense that human progress was slowing down. Trees do not grow to the sky, and the great march of industry and empire had to run out eventually. Perhaps a growing sense of what constituted normality and the redefinition of politics as the art of incremental improvements reflect that turn of events. It contrasts with the triumphal Romantic vision of human beings transcending everything they have been in the past: it is a kind of meek capitulation, a grey realism that, perhaps, suited the war-torn, polluted, anxious, bureaucratic, petty-bourgeois Victorian age. As the Romantics had come to believe that madness offered the possibility of genius, the Victorians learned that something called 'normality' could serve as its opposite without thereby being devalued. Stability, efficiency and utility came to be valued above mysterious supposed 'insights' that often seemed to lead them only to ingenuous mystical absurdities. In the process the quality the Romantics venerated as 'sublime' was pushed aside; yet in Machen and some of his contemporaries it rears its head again in just those places where normality seems to have taken the strongest hold.

The word 'sublime' literally means 'high up', and reminds us that low-high metaphors are weirdly contradictory in Western culture: high-minded people have deep thoughts and the highest wisdom is also the most profound. The metaphor of heights comes from the traditions of both Moses and Plato, where ascent towards heaven – usually by climbing a mountain – is the key metaphor for enlightenment. The climb is arduous but the view it affords is increasingly complete, encyclopædic, even God-like. This is reversed in the Augustinian world-view, in which true enlightenment is found not in the outdoors but through an inner, personal spiritual journey. It is here, in the fourth century, not in the Renaissance as some cultural historians assert, that the modern individual is born. Augustine's theology of grace is one of the foundation-stones of the Western cultural inheritance, and it paints redemption as a struggle that takes place within each believer. From now on, when the ascent of a mountain is an allegory of salvation – as in Bunyan's *Pilgrim's Progress*, for example – it is always implicit that the height is really a depth, the depth of the soul itself. It is here that the modern obsession with self-knowledge begins and that the individual as the unit of currency for all things spiritual, scientific, socio-economic and political is first struck.

It will not be surprising, then, to find that the heights of the sublime, as it emerges in the eighteenth century, will in fact be depths, or that the magnificence of nature 'in the large' will be a mere analogy for the magnificence of which each human soul – or at least that of the genius – is capable. This is a case of what the Ancient Greeks called *ekstasis* – literally, to stand outside oneself: the soul of the individual is externalised in order to be encountered authentically. It's a contradictory motion: pushing something outside us as a way to bring it closer. We do this precisely when, in the Age of Enlightenment, we have come to see knowledge as a problem about getting what is radically outside us inside, crossing (if such a thing is possible) the Kantian divide between the contents of the mind and the mysterious, shadowy noumena, the little gods of the Real.

Far from transforming the extraordinary into the mundane, far from a movement of bringing the strange and heterogeneous under a system of simple laws, the experience of early modern science seems to have been one of wonder. The wonders of distant lands, as improbably recounted by travellers like Sir John Mandeville; the extraordinary sights that can be seen through the telescope, recounted by Galileo, and later the microscope as described in Hooke's bestseller; weird and ancient ethnological discoveries; strange new commodities and technologies. Yet Francis Bacon reduced science to a branch of the law and Descartes imagined nature as a machine, two quite different metaphors that remain current today. Bacon was a lawyer by profession, Descartes a physicist and engineer; both men may have been reacting to the anxieties the wonders of their age produced by making them mundane and familiar. For Machen, it will be the mundane that is the precise source of anxiety.

Yet before Bacon or Descartes, the mathematician Girolamo Cardano, in his *De subtilitate rerum* (1550), had tried to create a model of the emerging sciences that did not deny their capacity for wonder. Cardano is best remembered today for three things: his application of the complex numbers, involving the square root of -1, which he took far more seriously than those of his Greek and Indian predecessors who had noticed their existence; his very important work on probability, a field he more or less invented; and his colourful life, of gambling, mysticism, duelling and (alleged) plagiarism. *De subtilitate* is a monograph on the 'subtlety' that makes the ancient, complex, murky, distant or profound inaccessible to ordinary, casual intelligence. It is this subtle

Girolamo Cardano (1501-76)

knowledge that Cardano values most highly: it is that which cannot be grasped in the way that a beautiful thing can be grasped, all at once and with relative ease. Rather it requires struggle, and perhaps something more. Here and elsewhere Cardano alludes to the state of ecstasy reported by certain Christian mystics, a state that can include visions and other apparently supernatural experiences. Cardano is cautious and scientific: these effects, he points out, can be obtained through such protocols as fasting, sleep deprivation, meditation on religious themes and emotional duress, all of which are often practiced by those who experience these ecstasies. Yet he does not rule out the possibility that the 'knowledge' they bestow – directly, in a flash of experience rather than by argument – may be true. The enthusiasm of the mystic might be a bridge to knowledge of the divine things that lie on the other side of Lessing's Ditch, things that are inaccessible to experiment. In Burton's *Anatomy of Melancholy* (1620), this part of Cardano's discussion has already become embarrassing and been abandoned: now it is the task of the sober Protestant thinker to debunk these popish illusions for what they are.

At one level, Cardano's ideas merely expressed a common pattern of sixteenth century thought: that some knowledge, the most hidden and hence 'occult', required great subtlety and wisdom to access and could not be discovered by the mere brute force of observation. This subtle way of knowing included mathematical methods, philosophical reflection, theology, metaphysics and magical thinking. It was mysterious, at least in part because its practitioners hid it from the light; perhaps they did so to preserve their monopoly on it, or perhaps because their achievements were considerably smaller than their rhetoric let on. The proto-scientists of the dog days of the alchemists did make genuine discoveries using methods not far away from what would today be considered scientific, yet they also made many gross errors. They allowed their ambitions to run away with them until eventually their self-aggrandisement wore thin. In the seventeenth century 'subtle' wisdom would go out of fashion among the intellectuals, relegated to tawdry popular supernaturalism and the ecstasies of religious mania. At another level, though, Cardano's ideas were untimely: he had hit on something that would not re-emerge in intellectual spheres for a century and a half. When it did, it would have a new name: the 'sublime'.

Edmund Burke was the most famous (but by no means the first) to define the sublime in his own time. In 1756 he wrote:

> Whatever is fitted in any sort to excite the ideas of pain and danger, that is to say, whatever is in any sort terrible, or is conversant about terrible objects, or operates in a manner analogous to terror, is a source of the sublime; that is, it is productive of the strongest emotion which the mind is capable of feeling.

He describes its effects on the one who experiences it:

> The passion caused by the great and sublime in nature, when those causes operate most powerfully, is astonishment; and astonishment is that state of the soul, in which all its motions are suspended, with some degree of horror. In this case the mind is so entirely filled with its object, that it cannot entertain any other, nor by consequence reason on that object which employs it.

We must remember, reading these words, the wonder that infuses the practice and consumption of early modern science. We might also think of Cardano: here is a form of knowledge not acquired by the slow nibbling of the data-gatherers, the 'natural historians' Bacon had exhorted to build mountains of observation in the hope that this, on its own, would create knowledge. This is a momentary glimpse of something beyond rational apprehension: a rush of insight.

For Burke and his contemporaries these feelings contrast sharply with those aroused by the 'beautiful', which is to say, that which is orderly, poised, regular, symmetrical, civilised, polished, artificial and can be grasped all at once as a satisfying whole. That was the aesthetic of the Classicists, an aesthetic that gave us delicate sensibilities, not raging *Sturm und Drang*. By Burke's time it is the aesthetic of patterned china plates and flock wallpaper, the aesthetic of calm, pleasing domesticity. It persisted as an idea, for it was clear enough that people do find pleasure in such things.

If the beautiful had a calming effect, the sublime could be disruptive. It was that which was too large, too high, too deep or too ancient to be 'framed' by the rational mind: later it would be painted as something literally too large to fit onto the canvas, as in Caspar David Friedrich's mountains or Goya's *Colossus*. That which is sublimely vast is so only because it defeats our capacity for conceiving of it; that which is sublimely ancient, tempestuous or profound has the same quality. In other words, as Derrida argued in response to Kant's account, it is our failure to measure the cosmos by our own standards that gives rise to the unique experience of the sublime. While the beautiful is given to us by positive qualities, the sublime is above all a falling-short, a negative moment in which the noumenal world reveals itself by exceeding our mental capacities to render it as a phenomenon. The sublime is that which we cannot experience being, paradoxically, experienced. It brings that which is radically outside us in, but only as a negative trace or fragment.

'Ecstasy' is the word that the hermit in Machen's *Hieroglyphics* uses to distinguish 'fine literature' as categorically separate from other kinds of writing. The idea of stepping outside oneself contained in the Greek word *ekstasis* unifies many of the themes we find in Machen's work: the experience of the sublime; the 'true seeing' that he gets from Goethe and Coleridge; the traces of pantheism; the mysticism. *Ekstasis* was the word used to describe the *maenads*, or 'the raving ones', the female retinue of Dionysus (or the Roman Bacchus). If humans do not give tribute to the god, the *maenad* brings them under her spell, and in her frenzy leaves them in chaos, dancing until they lose their senses in a frenzy of howling drunken sexual abandon. The *maenads'* wild behaviour was often considered a threat to the ordered life of the Greek *polis*. This was, perhaps, the kind of hysteria Plato was concerned about when he banned the poets from his utopian Republic.

Yet ecstasy is a temporary state. It offers a momentary escape from normality (and, in extreme cases, reality), after which we are expected to return to this world. Literature may have offered a kind of ecstasy to its readers, but it was a rather mild and fleeting one. On the other hand, literary men throughout the nineteenth century clung to the Romantic conflation of genius with insanity. If they could not obtain madness by ordinary means, many did so through the dissociative properties of alcohol or opium. One of John Haslam's cases concerned a 64-year-old man, 'R. B.', who described himself as a poet and appeared to be suffering under the rather literary delusion that he was actually the ancient Greek poet Anacreon. The man had been admitted to Bedlam having nearly killed himself with excessive drinking – he only lived another three months – but whether the alcohol had damaged his mind, or whether he had been driven to drink by his madness, was unknown. Anacreon was an appropriate choice: the poet was known for composing drinking songs, love poetry and the hymns to Dionysus called 'dithyrambs'. Some of his poetry had been published in the seventeenth century in English translations, including a few by Herrick. At about the same time Haslam was treating 'R. B.', Thomas Moore was publishing his translations of Anacreon, which include an ode that begins:

> I pray thee, by the gods above,
> Give me the mighty bowl I love,
> And let me sing, in wild delight,
> "I will - I will be mad tonight!"
> Alcmæon once, as legends tell,
> Was frenzied by the fiends of hell;
> Orestes too, with naked tread,
> Frantic pac'd the mountain-head;
> And why? a murder'd mother's shade
> Before their conscious fancy play'd.
> But I can ne'er a murderer be,
> The grape alone shall bleed by me;
> Yet can I rave, in wild delight,
> "I will - I will be mad tonight."

The poets who wanted to be mad did so because madness meant genius. Byron – famously 'mad, bad and dangerous to know' – behaved with outrageous disdain for others but it was probably a mixture of public performance and the entitled selfishness that comes of extraordinary privilege. Shelley and Keats were both obsessed with Gothic imagery, cultivated their highly-strung nerves and brooded overmuch on death, but it is not clear whether either would be diagnosed with any mental illness today. Much of it was probably affectation, and certainly others laboriously imitated them.

High Romanticism could not outlast its generation: it quickly lost the sharp edge of newness and fell into familiar pastiche. Those who followed leaned more heavily on their predecessors' technical brilliance than their sensibilities. Tennyson, Browning, the Rossettis and the rest wrote a poetry that was at once more stately, more serious, more ambitious and less individualistic.

One of the most intense of these mid-century poets, Algernon Charles Swinburne, lived at 3 Great James Street. One day his neighbour, Theodore Watts-Dunton, who lived at number 15, called with a letter of introduction. Watts-Dunton was a solicitor to Rossetti, a minor poet, and a camp-follower of the Pre-Raphaelites. He 'surprised Swinburne in a state of undress, and was chased onto the pavement by a furious naked poet', David Hayes tells us, 'but nevertheless befriended the poet and set about rescuing him from his life of debauchery'. This illustrates the shift: his 'debauchery' is no longer seen as an integral part to his genius. By this time it was no longer *de rigeur* to knock back claret or laudanum in order to access some transcendental madness in which the truth might be discerned. Moments of ecstasy might be sought out, but they begin to take on a negative sheen: they are ways to escape the intellectual work of writing, not routes to a primordial source. The actual writing of poetry begins to be staged in the cold light of normality, even where it looked back towards a more authentic genius lost to the past.

The poetry of a generation later had become still more nostalgic: Hardy and Yeats, in their own ways, turned to the past for both a literature and a form of life that were more authentic than anything possible under modernity. Yeats's contemporary Ernest Dowson lodged at 1 Guilford Place in the late nineteenth century; he is best remembered for vivid phrases, some of which (from 'Vitae Summa Brevis', 1896) have passed into the language:

> They are not long, the days of wine and roses:
> Out of a misty dream
> Our path emerges for a while, then closes
> Within a dream.

Other lines (from 'Non Sum Qualis Eram Bonae Sub Regno Cynarae', 1894) provided a title for something now rather more famous:

> I have forgot much, Cynara! gone with the wind,
> Flung roses, roses riotously with the throng,
> Dancing, to put thy pale, lost lilies out of mind;
> But I was desolate and sick of an old passion,
> Yea, all the time, because the dance was long:
> I have been faithful to thee, Cynara! in my fashion.

The poet is permanently separated from the wholeness represented by his beloved by an uncrossable ditch; nonetheless he tries, unsuccessfully, to be 'faithful to thee in my fashion'. The Dionysian ecstasy celebrated by Anacreon, now an indistinct dream, is indeed gone with the wind.

John Keats, while a medical student at Guy's Hospital, may have pondered the strange separation between the lifeless cadavers set out before him and the maelstrom of thought lashing through his mind. His mentor, John Spurgin, wrote earnest letters to the poet encouraging him to read another dreamer of ecstatic dreams: Emanuel Swedenborg. Dr Spurgin, a physician to the Foundling Hospital, went on to become Chairman of the Swedenborg Society; he lived for many years at 38 Guilford Street.

In Machen's *The Three Impostors*, Dyson is shaken up by a violent incident in which he glimpses 'the shadows of hidden forms, chasing and hurrying, and grasping and vanishing across the bright curtain of common life'. He hurriedly makes his way out of the 'sour and squalid quarter' of London he had wandered into, and 'emerging at Gray's Inn Road, struck off down Guilford Street and hastened home, only anxious for a lighted candle and solitude'.

If, in 2013, you follow in Dyson's footsteps, 150 years after Machen's birth, and make your way up Guilford Street, from Gray's Inn Road at its east end to Russell Square in the west, you can still see an off-white band running between ground and first floor on many of the original eighteenth-century houses, now home to small hotels and offices for universities. This feature runs the entire length of Guilford Street. This was the invention of Samuel Pepys Cockerell, surveyor to the Foundling Estate, charged with upholding architectural integrity across the numerous leasehold contracts with builders who bricked up Fanny Burney's sylvan view forever. It is his 'stone string' which at one point ran continuously from west to east, its purpose to disguise the gradual degradation from first-rate to fourth-rate houses. The purpose of the stone string was to tie together disparate things; it gave them a kind of unity, even if it was a false one. Today only the careful observer will notice it, since it can only be seen in fragments.

In this book we have surveyed a number of very different ideas – madness, childhood, reason, folklore, music, ecstasy, mysticism, science; all of which have been held by some to allow passage beyond the veil of perception. There are parallels between what we have found and Cockerell's stone string. Notions of what exactly *is* veiled, and how to unveil it, have been fragmentary and must be reconstructed in order to be understood. The ideas run out of sight for a while before re-emerging in unexpected places. You can walk them past every day without really noticing them. In our reconstruction, though, we must be on our guard not to create an overly tidy world-view out of incompatible traditions or contradictory philosophies, otherwise we are little better than the Victorian 'restorers' of mediæval buildings that recast history in their own tastes, causing untold damage and attracting the ire of William Morris.

For Machen, the search for this mysterious passage characterised his own spiritual life as much as it defined the kind of literature to which he aspired:

> Fragments of Samuel Pepys Cockerell's 'stone string' lace together what remains of eighteenth-century Guilford Street.

> literature depends upon this faculty of seeing the universe, from the æonian pebble of the wayside to the raw suburban street as something new, unheard of, marvellous, finally, miraculous. (*Far Off Things*, 1922)

Machen claimed that the touchstone of literature could be encapsulated in one word – ecstasy: 'substitute, if you like, rapture, beauty, adoration, wonder, awe, mystery, sense of the unknown, desire for the unknown'. He found this quality in Charles Dickens, but thought that Dickens

> ludicrously misinterprets his own *Pickwick*. And, doubtless, this understanding of the artificer of the artist varies in an almost infinite chain of nuances: there have been artists, perhaps, who have worked like men under

the influence of haschish, who have opened their mouths and prophesied, and then recovering from the possession, have sat up and stared, and asked where they were, and what they had been doing. Indeed, it may be that this was the condition of the working of art in the very dawn of human life, for this, no doubt, is the explanation of that old equation in which bards, magicians, seers, prophets, and madmen ranked all together as men who spoke and worked miracles...

In 'N', Machen invents a writer, the Reverend Thomas Hampole, and in his imaginary book-within-a-book (*A London Walk: Meditations in the Streets of the Metropolis*), his eyes glitter with revelation:

> Has it ever been your fortune... to rise in the earliest dawning of a summer day, ere yet the radiant beams of the sun have done more than touch with light the domes and spires of the great city? ...have you not observed that magic powers have apparently been at work? The accustomed scene has lost its familiar appearance. The houses which you have passed daily, it may be for years... now seem as if you beheld them for the first time. They have suffered a mysterious change, into something rich and strange... They have become magical habitations, supernal dwellings, more desirable to the eye than the fabled pleasure dome of the Eastern potentate, or the bejewelled hall built by the Genie for Aladdin in the Arabian tale.

The Reverend steps outside of his Anglican sensibilities into Renaissance magic.

> Some have declared that it lies within our own choice to gaze continually upon a world of equal or even greater wonder and beauty. The experiments of the alchemists of the Dark Ages are related, not to the transmutation of metals, but to the transmutations of the entire Universe to restore the delights of the primal Paradise; to enable men, if they will, to inhabit a world of joy and splendour. It is perhaps possible that there is such an experiment, and that there are some who have made it.

It requires a leap, over Lessing's broad ugly ditch. Science and reason skid to an abrupt halt at the edge. What if you don't make it to the other side, and all that lies within the ditch is madness and terror? What if there is no other side? For the

Romantics, children can make the leap into other worlds because they have not yet learned that fear; the mad can do so because they have forgotten it. For the rest, they think, it requires something like faith.

Machen populates this ditch with monstrous beings, grotesque and fantastic shapes, omens of confusion and disorder, threats of madness; a strange company from another world. They symbolise that fear of leaping. Lucian encounters the ecstasy of the *maenads* in *The Hill of Dreams:* the street orgy, the naphtha lamps, the black shadows, the roar of voices, where he meets the tall and lovely young woman with a 'strange look as of an old picture in her face'. He flees in terror of making the leap: 'he knew that he had touched the brink of utter desolation'.

We still want for uncontroversial accounts of what it means to be rational or to pursue a scientific enquiry correctly. Two centuries after psychology was put on an empirical footing, we are more confused than ever as to the distinction – if there is any – between madness and sanity. We do not know the status of our knowledge, or whether certain knowledge is possible. We do not even know whether the world we experience is like the world as it really is, or what it would even mean to answer such a question. We have been unable to discover universally valid moral laws or laws of taste: indeed, we believe in them less than ever, although we continue to firmly resist the relativism that that implies. We still feel threatened by absorption into a faceless 'mass' of humanity and as a consequence we praise individual genius. Such things are tantalising, like Machen's otherworldly yearning; it is a desire not for something radically separated from us but for something present yet inaccessible, something we cannot make out despite its being right before our eyes. For Machen, the ditch is monstrous, but the leap itself is ecstasy. Other characters make this leap, with serene grace: Edward Darnell in *A Fragment of Life* experiences a shining of light within his eyes and upon his face, 'as if for him the veil grew thin and soon would disappear'.

A veil allows you to see and prevents you from seeing at the same time; in Latin it was sometimes known as an *integumentum*, a covering or skin. In the eighteenth century German writers like Lessing translated the Greek word *mythos* as *Fabel*, fable; they called myths *integumenti*, sugar-coatings on the bitter pill of truth they contained. Myth reveals the truth by veiling it. The fragments of ideas that we have written about resist a methodical, analytical approach to history, yet at the same time it has not been our wish to conjure up the illusion of a veil, behind which historical Truth can be found, revealed by means of concealment.

Nor do we invite you to embrace a hidden Truth by making such an ecstatic leap; although, as the Reverend Hampole admits, it is perhaps possible that there is such an experiment, and that there are some who have made it. But however sceptical we may be, that gesture would appear to be the only kind available to us when simple logic fails.

But there is a middle way. We believe that we should not turn our backs on the complexity and contradictions of these fragments in favour of a simplified, homogenous story that leaves too much out. Machen's way of looking at the world and at literature offered a strategy for coping with this. As a matter of fact, it's not a bad way of coming to terms with the vastness of London. The surface of the city can by turns be grimy, pompous and trivial, presenting a series of scenes which inspire revulsion or despair. Machen sought instead what he called the light glowing behind grey material walls – living stones, quickening and palpitating – of hues that the mortal eye had never seen – hinting at the deeper beauty of the city in all its contradictions. The danger of such a view is complacency. As Machen himself realised, one must resist the deceptions of mysticism, the promise of what Adorno called 'the cheap utopia, the false utopia, the utopia that can be bought'. We must similarly resist the temptation to produce a sanitised, unified, picturesque, glorified image of London and its past. It may be possible to chalk a magic square of any size around London and find infinite stories, much like Darwin in his twilight years would set out squares in his garden, a yard by a yard, and trace in wonder the lives of earthworms, in whom he found quiet mysteries that seemed to symbolise his life's work.

BIBLIOGRAPHY

Abrams, M.H. (1953) *The Mirror and the Lamp: Romantic Theory and the Critical Tradition*. Oxford: Oxford University Press.
Adams, J. (2001) *Madder Music, Stronger Wine: The Life of Ernest Dowson, Poet and Decadent*. London: Tauris Parke Paperbacks
Addison, J. (1709) 'From my own apartment, May 20', in *The Tatler*, No. 18.
Adorno, T. and Bloch, E. (1988) 'Something's missing', in J. Zipes and F. Mechlenburg (trans.) *The Utopian Function of Art and Literature: Selected Essays*. Cambridge: Massachusetts Institute of Technology.
Anthony, P.D. (1983) *John Ruskin's Labour: A Study of Ruskin's Social Theory*. Cambridge: Cambridge University Press.
Aristotle (1986) *De Anima*, trans. H. Lawson-Tancred. London: Penguin.
Armenteros, C. (2011) *The French Idea of History: Joseph de Maistre and his Heirs, 1794-1854*. Ithaca, NY: Cornell University Press.
Arnold, M. (1867) *On the Study of Celtic Literature*. London: Smith, Elder & Co.
– (1914) *Essays*. Oxford: Oxford University Press.
Arteaga, J.R. (2004) 'The constitutionality of the insanity defense: a comprehensive examination of the insanity defense in a historical and contemporary context', in McGee (ed.), *Commentaries on Law and Public Policy, Vol. 2*. Miami, Fl.: Dumont Institute for Public Policy Research.
Baker, G. & Morris, K.J. (1996) *Descartes' Dualism*. London: Routledge.
Ball, M. & Sunderland, D. (2001) *An Economic History of London 1800-1914*. London: Routledge.
Barthes, R. (1990) *A Lover's Discourse*, trans. R. Howard. London: Penguin.
Bartók, B. (1976) *Essays*, ed. B. Suchoff. New York: St. Martin's Press.
Beiser, F.C. (2002) *German Idealism: The Struggle Against Subjectivism, 1781-1801*. Cambridge, MA: Harvard University Press.
– (2009) *Diotima's Children: German Aesthetic Rationalism from Leibniz to Lessing*. Oxford: Oxford University Press.
– (1987) *The Fate of Reason: German Philosophy from Kant to Fichte*. Cambridge, MA: Harvard University Press.
Bøggild, J. (2006) 'Reflections of Kierkegaard in the tales of Hans Christian Andersen', in *Kierkegaard Studies Yearbook 2006*.

Bonds, M.E. (1998) 'Haydn's "Cours complet de la composition" and the Sturm und Drang' in Sutcliffe, W.D. (ed.), *Haydn Studies*. Cambridge: Cambridge University Press.

Bowman, F.P. (1984) 'Illuminism, utopia, mythology' in D.G. Charlton (ed.) *The French Romantics Vol 1*. Cambridge: Cambridge University Press.

Boyle, R. (1685) *Essay of the Great Effects of Even Languid and Unheeded Motion*. London: Richard Davis.

Brown, F.B. (2000) *Good Taste, Bad Taste and Christian Taste: Aesthetics in Religious Life*. Oxford: Oxford University Press.

Browning, R. (1887) *Parleyings with Certain People of Importance in their Day*. London: Smith, Elder & Co.

Buch, D.J. (2008) *Magic Flutes and Enchanted Forests: The Supernatural in Eighteenth-Century Musical Theatre*. Chicago, Ill.: University of Chicago Press.

Bunzl, M. (1996) 'Franz Boas and the Humboldtian tradition', in G.W. Stocking Jr (ed.) *Volksgeist as Method and Ethic: Essays on Boasian Ethnography and the German Anthropological Tradition*. Madison, WI: University of Wisconsin Press.

Burke, E. (1764) *A Philosophical Enquiry into the Origin of our Ideas of the Sublime and Beautiful*. London: R. & J. Dodsley.

Bywely, A. (1997) *Realism, Representation and the Arts in Nineteenth Century Literature*. Cambridge: Cambridge University Press.

Campbell, J. (1748) *Hermippus Redivivus*. London: J. Nourse.

Cheyne, G. (1733) *The English Malady*. London: G. Strahan.

Coleridge, S.T. (1817) *Biographia Literaria*. London: Rest Fenner.

Comte, A. (1858) *The Catechism of Positive Religion*, trans. R. Congreve. London: John Chapman.

— (1988) *Introduction to Positive Philosophy*, ed. F. Ferré. Indianapolis, IN: Hackett.

Condorcet A.-N. de (1955) *Sketch for a Historical Picture of the Progress of the Human Mind*, trans. J. Barraclough. London: Weidenfeld & Nicholson.

Constantine, M. (2007) *The Truth Against the World: Iolo Morganwg and Romantic Forgery*. Cardiff: University of Wales Press.

Cooper, A.A. (Earl of Shaftesbury) (1904) *An Inquiry Concerning Virtue or Merit*. Heidelberg: Carl Winter.

Curtis, B. (2008) *Music Makes the Nation: Nationalist Composers and Nation-Building in Nineteenth-Century Europe*. Amherst, NY: Cambria Press.

Dailey, D. and Tomedi, J. (2005) *London (Blooms Literary Places)*, London: Chelsea House Publishers

D'Amico, D. (1999) *Christina Rossetti: Faith, Gender and Time*. Baton Rouge, LA: Louisiana State University Press.

D'Arblay, F. (1832) *Memoirs of Dr. Burney*. London: Edward Moxon.

Darnton, R. (1968) *Mesmerism and the End of the Enlightenment in France*. Cambridge, MA.: Harvard University Press.

Davies, R. (2001) *Descartes: Belief, Scepticism and Virtue*. London: Routledge.

Davis, T.W. (2004) *Shifting Sands: The Rise and Fall of Biblical Archæology*. Oxford: Oxford University Press.

Dearnley, M. (1968) *The Poetry of Christopher Smart*. London: C. Tinling.

Derrida, J. (1987) *The Truth in Painting*. Chicago: University of Chicago Press.
Descartes, R. (1968) *Discourse on Method and the Meditations,* trans. F. E. Sutcliffe. London: Penguin.
Downes, S. (2001) 'Eros and paneuropeanism: Szymanowski's utopian vision', in H. White & M. Murphy (ed.) *Constructions of Nationalism: Essays on the History and Ideology of European Musical Culture 1800-1945*. Cork: Cork University Press.
Ebeling, F. (2007) *The Secret History of Hermes Trismegistus: Hermeticism from Ancient to Modern*, trans. D. Lorton. Itheca, NY: Cornell University Press.
Eitner, L. (1972) *Géricault's Raft of the Medusa*. London: Phaidon.
Eliot, C.W. (1909) 'Introductory note', in *Folklore and Fable: Aesop, Grimm, Andersen*. New York: P.F. Collier & Son.
Ellis, M. (1996) *The Politics of Sensibility: Race, Gender and Commerce in the Sentimental Novel*. Cambridge: Cambridge University Press.
Erskine, T. (1870) *The Speeches of Thomas Erskine, Vol. 2*. London: Reeves & Turner.
Falkenberg, M. (2005) *Rethinking the Uncanny in Hoffmann and Tieck*. Bern: Peter Lang.
Ferrari, G.R.F. (2005) *City and Soul in Plato's Republic*. Chicago, Ill.: University of Chicago Press.
Ferriar, J. (1813) *An Essay Towards a Theory of Apparitions*. London: Cadell & Davies.
Finger, S. (2006) *Dr Franklin's Medicine*. Philadelphia, Penn.: University of Pennsylvania Press.
Force, J.E. (1990) 'Hume's interest in Newton and science', in J.E. Force & R.H. Popkin, *Essays on the Context, Nature, and Influence of Isaac Newton's Theology*. Dordrecht: Kluwer.
Foucault, M. (1989) *The Birth of the Clinic: An Archæology of Medical Perception*, trans. A.M. Sheridan. London: Routledge.
– (2006) *Psychiatric Power: Lectures at the Collège de France, 1973-1974*, trans. G. Burchell. Basingstoke: Palgrave Macmillan.
Foyster, E. (2002) 'Creating a veil of silence? Politeness and marital violence in the English household' in *Transactions of the Royal Historical Society*, Series 6 Vol. 12.
Freud, S. (1949) *Three Essays on the Theory of Sexuality*, trans. Strachey. Oxford: Imago.
Gaier, U. (2009) 'Myth, mythology, new mythology', in H. Adler & W. Kèopke (ed.) *A Companion to the Works of Johann Gottfried Herder*. Rochester, NY: Camden House.
Gallo, D.A. & Finger, S. (2000) 'The power of a musical instrument: Franklin, the Mozarts, Mesmer and the glass armonica', in *History of Psychology*, 3:4.
Gantet, C. (2007) 'Dreams, standards of knowledge and orthodoxy in Germany in the sixteenth century', in R.C. Head & D. Christensen (ed.) *Orthodoxies and Heterodoxies in Early Modern German Culture: Order and Creativity 1550-1750*. Leiden: Brill.
Giddens, A. (1982) *Profiles and Critiques in Social Theory*. Berkeley: University of California Press.
Giles, J. (2004) *The Parlour and the Suburb: Domestic Identities, Class, Femininity and Modernity*. Oxford: Berg.
Gill, M.B. (2006) *The British Moralists on Human Nature and the Birth of Secular Ethics*. Cambridge: Cambridge University Press.
Godfrey, W.H. and Marcham, W.McB. (editors) (1952) *Survey of London: volume 24: The parish of St Pancras part 4: King's Cross Neighbourhood*. London: English Heritage
Goethe, J.W. von (1840) *Theory of Colours*, trans. C.L. Eastlake. London: John Murray.

Goodrick-Clarke, N. (2008) *The Western Esoteric Traditions: A Historical Introduction.* Oxford: Oxford University Press.

Gould, G.M. & Pyle, W.L. (1896) *Anomalies and Curiosities of Medicine.* Philadelphia, Penn.: W.B. Saunders.

Gower, B. (1997) *Scientific Method: A Historical and Philosophical Introduction.* London: Routledge.

Grafton, A. (1991) *Defenders of the Text: The Traditions of Scholarship in an Age of Science, 1450-1800.* Cambridge, MA: Harvard University Press.

— (1999) *Cardano's Cosmos: The Worlds and Works of a Renaissance Astrologer.* Cambridge, MA: Harvard University Press.

Grainger, P. (1999) *Grainger on Music,* ed. M. Gillies & B.C. Ross. Oxford: Oxford University Press.

Green, I. (2009) *Humanism and Protestantism in Early Modern English Education.* Farnham: Ashgate.

Griesinger, W. (1867) *Mental Pathology and Therapeutics,* trans. Robertson & Rutherford. London: New Sydenham Society.

Hacking, I. (1990) *The Taming of Chance.* Cambridge: Cambridge University Press.

Hankins, T.L. & Silverman, R.J. (1999) *Instruments and the Imagination.* Princeton, NJ: Princeton University Press.

Harding, A.J. (1985) *Coleridge and the Inspired Word.* Montreal: McGill-Queen's University Press.

Haslam, J. (1809) *Observations on Madness and Melancholy.* London: J. Callow.

Hawes, C. (1996) *Mania and Literary Style: The Rhetoric of Enthusiasm from the Ranters to Christopher Smart.* Cambridge: Cambridge University Press.

Hayes, D. (1998) *East of Bloomsbury.* London: Camden Historic Society.

Hegel, G.W.F. (1967) *Philosophy of Right,* trans. T. M. Knox. Oxford: Oxford University Press.

Heidegger, M. (1977) *The Question Concerning Technology and Other Essays,* trans. W. Lovitt. New York: Harper & Row.

Hensel, H. (1998) 'Goethe, Science and Sensory Experience' in D. Seamon & A. Zajonc (ed.) *Goethe's Way of Science: A Phenomenology of Nature.* New York: SUNY Press.

Herder, J.G. (2006) *Selected Writings on Aesthetics,* trans. G. Moore. Princeton, NJ: Princeton University Press.

— (1803) *Outlines of a Philosophy of the History of Man,* trans. T. Churchill. London: J. Johnson.

Hibbert, C. (1977) *The Court at Windsor: A Domestic History.* London: Penguin.

Hill, R.G. (1839) 'Moral treatment of insanity' in *The Lancet,* July 6 1839.

— (1839) *Total Abolition of Personal Restraint in the Treatment of the Insane.* London: Simpkin, Marshall & Co.

Howell, T.B. (1820) *Howell's State Trials, Vol. XXVII.* London: T. C. Hansard.

Hudson, N. (1994) *Writing and European Thought, 1600-1830.* Cambridge: Cambridge University Press.

Hume, D. (2007) *An Enquiry Concerning Human Understanding,* ed. P. Millican. Oxford: Oxford University Press.

Hutcheson, F. (1742) *An Essay on the Nature and Conduct of the Passions and Affections, with Illustrations on the Moral Sense.* London: W. Innys.

— (1726) *An Inquiry into the Original of our Ideas of Beauty and Virtue.* London: J. Darby.

Hutchinson, W. (1775) *The Spirit of Masonry in Moral and Elucidatory Lectures.* London: J. Wilkie.

Ireland, J. (1812) *Hogarth Illustrated from his own Manuscripts.* London: Boydell & Co.
Jacobs, J.W. (1988) 'Euripides' Medea: a psychodynamic model of severe divorce pathology' in *American Journal of Psychotherapy* 42:2.
Kant, I. (1996) *Critique of Pure Reason,* trans. W.S. Pluhar. Indianapolis, IN: Hackett.
Kepler, J. (1997) *The Harmony of the World,* trans. Aiton, Duncan, Field. Philadelphia, Penn.: American Philosophical Society.
Kierkegaard, S. (2009) 'From the papers of one still living', in J. Watkins (ed.) *Kierkegaard's Writings I: Early Polemical Writings.* Princeton, NJ: Princeton University Press.
Killen, A. (2006) *Berlin Electropolis: Shock, Nerves and German Modernity.* Berkeley: University of California Press.
Kopans, D.G. (2006) *The English Malady: Engendering Insanity in the Eighteenth Century.* Unpublished PhD thesis, Carnegie Mellon University.
Lacan, J. (1981: 1993) *The Seminar of Jacques Lacan, Book III: The Psychoses, 1955-1956.* New York: W.W. Norton.
Lanska, D.J. & Lanska, J.T. (2007) 'Franz Anton Mesmer and the rise and fall of animal magnetism: dramatic cures, controversy and ultimately a triumph for the scientific method' in Whitaker et al. (ed.), *Mind, Brain and Medicine: Essays in Eighteenth-Century Neuroscience.* New York: Springer.
Leibniz, G.W. (1989) *Philosophical Essays,* trans. R. Ariew & D. Garber. Indianapolis, IN: Hackett.
Lessing, G. (1956) *Lessing's Theological Writings,* trans. H. Chadwick. Stanford, CA: Stanford University Press.
Lewis, P.E. (1996) *Seeing Through the Mother Goose Tales: Visual Turns in the Writings of Charles Perrault.* Stanford, CA: Stanford University Press.
Lippmann, E. (1992) *A History of Western Musical Aesthetics.* Lincoln, NE: University of Nebraska Press.
Loewen, H. (1974) *Luther and the Radicals.* Ontario: Wilfrid Laurier University.
Lovecraft, H.P. (1991) *Tales of H.P. Lovecraft.* London: HarperCollins.
Luckhurst, R. (2002) *The Invention of Telepathy.* Oxford: Oxford University Press.
Lukacs, György (1971) *The Theory of the Novel,* trans. A. Bostock. Cambridge, MA: MIT Press.
MacClancy, J. (2013) *Anthropology in the Public Arena: Historical and Contemporary Contexts.* London: John Wiley & Sons.
Machen, A. (1894) *The Great God Pan and The Inmost Light.* London: John Lane.
– (1895) *The Three Impostors.* London: John Lane.
– (1937) quoted in *Authors Take Sides on the Spanish War.* London: The Left Review.
– (1988) *The Collected Arthur Machen.* London: Gerald Duckworth. ('N')
– (1913) *Hieroglyphics: A Note Upon Ecstasy in Literature.* New York: Mitchell Kennerley.
– (2010) *The Hill of Dreams.* Cardigan: Parthian Library of Wales.
– (2011) *The White People and Other Weird Stories.* London: Penguin. ('The Red Hand', 'The White People', 'A Fragment of Life', 'The Great Return', 'Out of the Earth', 'The Terror')
– (2013) *Far Off Things.* Caerleon: The Three Impostors.
Mangham, A. (2004) '"Murdered at the breast": maternal violence and the self-made man in popular Victorian culture' in *Critical Survey* 16:1.

Marback, R. (1999) *Plato's Dream of Sophistry*. Columbia, SC: University of South Carolina Press.
Martens, R. (2000) *Kepler's Philosophy and the New Astronomy*. Princeton, NJ: Princeton University Press.
Mayo, R. (1954) 'The contemporaneity of the Lyrical Ballads', in *Proceedings of the Modern Language Association* 69:3.
McClelland, C. (2012) *Ombra: Supernatural Music in the Eighteenth Century*. Lanham, MD: Lexington.
McGowan, D. (2012) *Voices of Unbelief: Documents from Atheists and Agnostics*. Santa Barbara: ABC-CLIO.
Mill, J.S. (1924) *The Autobiography of John Stuart Mill*. New York: Columbia University Press.
Millan-Zaibert, E. (2007) *Friedrich Schlegel and the Emergence of Romantic Philosophy*. New York: SUNY Press.
Morris, W. (1966) *The Collected Works of William Morris Vol 20: The Water of the Wondrous Isles*, ed. M. Morris. New York: Russell & Russell.
Mullan, J. (1988) *Sentiment and Sensibility: The Language of Feeling in the Eighteenth Century*. Oxford: Clarendon Press.
Murray, M. (1931) *The God of the Witches*. London: Sampson Low, Marston & Co.
Neumann, S. (1993) 'The Brothers Grimm as collectors and editors of German folktales', in D. Haase (ed.), *The Reception of Grimms' Fairy Tales: Responses, Reactions, Revisions*. Detroit, MI: Wayne State University Press.
Nichols, J. (1786) *Annotations to The Tatler, with Illustrations and Notes Historical, Biographical and Critical, in Six Volumes*. London: C. Bathurst et al.
Parrinder, G. (1973) 'The witch as victim', in Newell, V. (ed.), *The Witch Figure*. London: Routledge & Kegan Paul.
Peters, T.J. & Wilkinson, D. (2010) 'King George III and porphyria: a clinical re-examination of the historical evidence' in *History of Psychiatry Journal*, 21:1:81.
Pickering, M. (2009) *Auguste Comte: An Intellectual Biography*. Cambridge: Cambridge University Press.
Pierenkemper, T. & Tilly, R. (2004) *The German Economy During the Nineteenth Century*. Oxford: Berghahn.
Plato (1997) *Complete Works*, ed. Cooper. Indianapolis, IN: Hackett.
Purkiss, D. (1996) *The Witch in History: Early Modern and Twentieth-Century Representations*. London: Routledge.
Reid, D.M. (2002) *Whose Pharaohs? Archæology, Museums and Egyptian National Identity from Napoleon to World War I*. Berkeley: University of California Press.
Reid, N. (2006) *Coleridge, Form and Symbol*. Aldershot: Ashgate.
Rennie, N. (2011) 'Imaginary Bloomsbury: Dynamite and Peter Pan', unpublished paper from The Bloomsbury Project at UCL, 15 April 2011
Rhys, J. (1901) *Celtic Folklore: Welsh and Manx* (two volumes). Oxford: Clarendon Press.
Rockmore, T. (1992) *On Heidegger's Nazism and Philosophy*. Berkeley: University of California Press.
Rosen, E. (1970) 'Was Copernicus a Hermetist?' in R. H. Stuewer (ed.) *Historical and Philosophical Perspectives of Science, Vol V*. Oxford: Oxford University Press.
Ryder, F.G. & Browning, R.M. (ed.) (2002) *German Literary Fairy Tales*. New York: Continuum.

Scull, A. (1993) *Most Solitary of Afflictions: Madness and Society in Britain, 1700-1900*. New Haven, CT: Yale University Press.
— (2006) *The Insanity of Place / The Place of Insanity: Essays on the History of Psychiatry*. London: Routledge.
Seashore, C.E. (1919) *The Psychology of Musical Talent*. New York: Silver, Burdett & Co.
Shortt, S.E.D. (1986) *Victorian Lunacy: Michard M. Bucke and the Practice of Late Nineteenth-Century Psychiatry*. Cambridge: Cambridge University Press.
Smith, A. (1759) *The Theory of Moral Sentiments*. London: A. Millar.
Spinoza, B. de (1996) *Ethics,* trans. E. Curley. London: Penguin.
Stukeley, W. (1740) *Stonehenge, A Temple Restor'd to the British Druids*. London: W. Innys & R. Manby.
— (1724) *Itinerarium Curiosum*. London: William Stukeley.
Summerfield, G. & Downward, L. (2010) *New Perspectives on the European Bildungsroman*. London: Continuum.
Szczelkun, S.A. (1993) *The Conspiracy of Good Taste: William Morris, Cecil Sharp, Clough Williams-Ellis and the Repression of Working Class Culture in the 20th Century*. London: Working Press.
Tavernor, R. (2007) *Smoot's Ear: The Measure of Humanity*. New Haven, CT: Yale University Press.
Treitel, C. (2004) *A Science for the Soul: Occultism and the Genesis of the German Modern*. Baltimore, MD: Johns Hopkins University Press.
Vaccari, A. (2008) 'Legitimating the machine: the epistemological foundation of technological metaphor in the natural philosophy of René Descartes', in C. Zittel et al. (ed.) *Philosophies of Technology: Francis Bacon and his Contemporaries*. Leiden: Brill.
Van Sant, A.J. (1993) *Eighteenth Century Sensibility and the Novel: The Senses in Social Context*. Cambridge: Cambridge University Presss.
Vaughan Williams, R. (2008) 'Howland Medal Lecture', in D. Manning (ed.) *Vaughan Williams on Music*. Oxford: Oxford University Press.
Venbrux, E. & Meder, T. (2004) 'Authenticity as an analytic concept in folkloristics: a case of collecting folktales in Friesland', in *Etnofodor,* 17:1.2.
Walford, E. (1878), *Old and New London*. London: Cassell.
Wardhaugh, B. (2008) 'Formal causes and mechanical causes: the analogy of the musical instrument in late seventeenth-century natural philosophy', in Zittel C. et al. (ed.), *Philosophies of Technology: Francis Bacon and his Contemporaries*. Leiden: Koninklijke Brill.
Warner, M. (2003) *Signs and Wonders: Essays on Literature and Culture*. London: Chatto & Windus.
Weckowicz, T.E. & Liebel-Weckowicz, H.P. (1990) *A History of Great Ideas in Abnormal Psychology*. Amsterdam: Elsevier.
Wheeler, K. (1980) *Sources, Processes and Methods in Coleridge's Biographia Literaria*. Cambridge: Cambridge University Press.
Wingfield, P. (1992) *Janáček: Glagolitic Mass*. Cambridge: Cambridge University Press.
Winslow, F.B. (1843) *The Plea of Insanity, in Criminal Cases*. Boston, MA: Little & Brown.
— (1860) *On Obscure Diseases of the Brain and Disorders of the Mind*. Philadelphia, PA: Blanchard & Lee.
Wittgenstein, L. (2009) *Philosophical Investigations,* trans. G.E.M. Anscombe et al. London: Wiley Blackwell.

Wright, J.P. (1990) 'Metaphysics and physiology: mind, body and the animal economy in eighteenth century Scotland', in Stewart, M. A. (ed.), *Studies in the Philosophy of the Scottish Enlightenment*. Oxford: Oxford University Press.

Zemanová, M. (2002) *Janáček*. London: John Murray.

Zipes, J. (2006) *Fairy Tales and the Art of Seduction*. London: Routledge.

– (1988) 'Dreams of a better bourgeois life: the psychosocial origins of the Grimms' tales', in J.M. McGlathery (ed.) *The Brothers Grimm and Folktale*. Champaign, IL: University of Illinois Press.

Printed in Great Britain
by Amazon